African
Art
in
Needlework

Other Books by Leslie Tillett:

The Fall of the Aztecs
American Needlework 1776/1976
Wind on the Buffalo Grass
The Zoophabet Needlework Book

Leslie Tillett
African Art in Needlework

Thomas Y. Crowell, Publishers

Established 1834

New York

To obtain information on needlework kits for the designs in this book please write to The Stitchery, 204 Worcester Street, Wellesley, Massachusetts 02181

AFRICAN ART IN NEEDLEWORK. Copyright © 1979 by Leslie Tillett. All rights reserved. Printed in the United States of America. No part of this book may be used or reproduced in any manner whatsoever without written permission except in the case of brief quotations embodied in critical articles and reviews. For information address Thomas Y. Crowell, Publishers, 10 East 53rd Street, New York, N.Y. 10022. Published simultaneously in Canada by Fitzhenry & Whiteside Limited, Toronto.

FIRST EDITION

Designed by Andrew Roberts

Library of Congress Cataloging in Publication Data

Tillett, Leslie, Date
    African art in needlework.

    1. Needlework—Patterns.   2. Design, Decorative—Africa.   I. Title.
TT753.T53   746.4'4   78-3320
ISBN 0-690-01404-X

79 80 81 82 83 10 9 8 7 6 5 4 3 2 1

To Esther Doctorow

Contents

Introduction   xiii

Embroidery   1

Basic Stitches   11

The Projects   41

AFRICAN MAP   45
BENIN HEAD   46
BRONZE PATTERN   48
BRONZE FRINGE   50
BRONZE FLOWERS   52
WHITE SLAVER   54
BRONZE FISH   56
BURLAP FISH   58
BURLAP FISHSCALES   59
ROOSTER FEATHERS   60
FEATHER FRAME   62
BRONZE ROOSTER   64
BENIN LEOPARD   66
BENIN LEOPARD SPOT   69
NIGERIAN PUFF   70

NIGERIAN DOUBLE PURSE   72

NIGERIAN BEADED BAG   76

NIGERIAN BEADED CUIRASS   78

LAGOS RUG   80

CONGO MASK   82

BUSHMAN HUNT   84

LESOTHO LEAF   86

CHIEF'S FAN   88

PAPILLIO ZEBRANCUS   90

ORNITHOPTERA GIRAFFICUS   92

POLYGONIA LEOPARDUS   94

CHEETAH SKIN   97

AKAN QUILT   98

AKAN HAND PANEL   102

AKAN HEART PILLOW   103

AKAN FISH PILLOW   104

AKAN WHEEL PILLOW   105

AKAN LIZARD PILLOW   106

AKAN ELEPHANT PILLOW   107

KUBA RAFFIA PANEL   108

ZAIRE BARK FABRIC   113

OLOKUN ADIRE   116

GOLD COAST KENTE   119

LIBERIAN HUNTER   122

LIBERIAN HORSEMAN   125

LIBERIAN MASK PANEL   127

KENTE CLOTH   129

FON APPLIQUÉ   132

IBO APPLIQUÉ   134

Index

Index   137

Acknowledgments

I have had so much help here and in Africa that it would be impossible to list it all; however, to Bernice Barsky, who knows so much more about needlework technique than I ever will, go my real thanks, for her work made the book possible; to Vicky Negrin, who researched and took care of the home fort whilst I was in Africa, go also many thanks. Stacey Pennebaker patiently inked yards of diagrams with precision and Jean Olgeirson helped pull all together.

Introduction

The richly varied artworks of Sub-Saharan Africa are so great in number and so adaptable to needlework designs that the main problem was to cull out the best. I had constantly to remind myself that the designs were intended for needleworkers of differing levels of skill. Perhaps because of my textile background, I found the fabrics an enticing source of inspiration.

My travels in Africa have not been as extensive as my wanderings through the museums of the Americas and Europe. The group shown in this book represents both sources, but it cannot indicate all the cultures of Sub-Saharan Africa.

The work of African artists and artisans during the last 100 years is hard to find in Africa itself because it has been so heavily plundered by the colonial powers. However, as the museums of Europe and the private collections there begin to sell the loot to the Americans, more can be seen in this country.

When I am in Africa it is as a consultant on product design, so that I get little chance for more than a rough sketch. The drawings of the original sources shown here were therefore mostly worked up in my New York studio.

I have included pieces from New York City's Museum of Natural History, as well as from other museums such as the Field Museum of Chicago. One of the best exhibits of things African was the African Decorative Art Show at the Museum of Modern Art in 1972, where I made quite a few drawings that led to needlework designs shown here.

We outside Africa cannot hope to explain the wild originality of African art; indeed, such extravagance and grotesque beauty may never be fully understood. A simplistic reason for the bizarre forms of its plastic art is the perishable nature of the material used, which calls for continued replacement and so provides the opportunity of more frequent invention than the marble and stone of classical Greece and Rome.

Standing in the amazing bowl—many miles wide and fringed all round with contorted stone shapes—that is the center of a place called Sethslabatebe in the Kingdom of Lesotho, it is clear that no conventional work could come out of such an inspiration. Knowing that one is in or on the roof of Africa, 11,000 feet above the plains and surrounded by such forms, helps to explain the murals on cave walls made by Bushmen long ago; yet I was conscious also of all the preconceived African images I brought to that scene.

The outsider, even when born inside Africa, cannot know what forces generated African art. Perhaps Baroness Blixen, in her musings in *Out of Africa,* has come near to making us feel we understand. I hope this book will help a little more in that understanding and will lead Americans to search deeper in the future.

Embroidery

Ornamenting a surface with stitches is known as embroidery, whether it is done by hand or machine, for function or decoration. Although the needlework collected here was planned for experienced needleworkers, the importance of time—that is, of taking time for this process of embroidery—may not be fully appreciated.

Embroidery is stitching, but it is not sewing. The stitches should lie *on* the cloth or canvas, not in it. To accomplish this, you should always do one motion of a stitch at a time, completing each before going on to the next. The Running stitch, which everyone knows, can serve as a simple case in point: For this trial, fasten thread on the wrong side of the cloth. Bring needle through to the right side, drawing thread out as far as it will go; there should be no sign of pulling in the cloth. At desired length of stitch, take needle to the wrong side again. From the back of the work, draw thread out until the stitch has been eased in place on the cloth surface. Continue in this way for desired number of stitches. Note the use of the words "draw" and "ease" here—there should be no pulling in embroidery. And note also that the humble Running stitch has become a decoration. Try it in this way with a somewhat heavier thread for top-stitching the edge of a garment or a welted seam.

As with any stitching, there should be some tension in the cloth, and frames are helpful in maintaining it. These will be discussed under MATERIALS.

Tension should be only in the cloth, not in the thread or stitch. By taking time to execute stitches, you will find that they are controlled, not pulled taut. The cloth will not be gathered in, and the canvas will be less warped. Long, straight stitches, as in Bargello, will be more perfect.

Take time also to correct the twist of your working thread. From the normal motion of stitching, all threads overtwist and untwist. Allow the needle and thread to hang from the work so that its original twist can return. Do this frequently to avoid distorted or sloppy-looking stitches.

MATERIALS, EQUIPMENT

Canvas: Experienced needleworkers usually know the various types and gauges of canvas; recommended gauges are included here in the instructions for each canvas embroidery. But few people may know that canvas sizes are only nominal, not actual. Canvas supposed to be the same gauge, but cut from different bolts, will vary greatly. Although canvas is supposed to be square in weave, the warp (vertical threads) gauge is rarely identical to the weft (horizontal threads). Therefore, if a specific number of canvas threads in length and/or width is necessary for a project, *count them,* do not measure. Without counting, your canvas might be an inch or more too short.

Fabrics: The cloths used for these embroideries have been included in the materials listing. Of course substitutions can be made to suit your purpose; and almost any type of fabric can be embroidered.

However, if your chosen base cloth is quite textured, consider the use of a temporary sheer cloth over it for the needleworking. (See "Transferring Designs" to dark fabrics—p. 7—for the technique.) This will prevent raised surfaces from interfering with stitching, and will also prevent snagging the cloth. As described in "Transferring," the sheer cloth is raveled when the embroidery has been completed.

Knitted, sheer, or bias-cut cloth can be embroidered in the same way. This time the temporary sheer is used for stability. Or the reverse action can be taken. Use a sheer—such as organdie—as interfacing under the base cloth, stitching through both thicknesses as before. If your base fabric is very transparent, the interfacing should be of a similar tint. And in this case it need not be raveled after the work is through, unless so desired. Under a bias cut, keep the interfacing on the grain to prevent stretching.

Threads: The needlework in this book was stitched with Paternayan Persian wool and DMC Six-Strand Embroidery Cotton, either with single threads or in strands of several at a time. If you change the weight of fabrics suggested here, you may also want to change the thickness of threads used. For heavier cloths, consider using an additional thread or two per strand, and vice versa. Or consider, too, the several thicknesses of DMC Perle Cotton from No. 8 through No. 1, the heaviest.

If an embroidered article is likely to be laundered, make sure the threads can be. And if you plan to use some offbeat yarns, test them for colorfastness and perhaps even pre-shrink them. Wool may not be the best choice, for although many types are colorfast, some continue to shrink with each washing.

Needles: Just as nominal gauges of canvas are only approximate, so different brands of same-size needles may not actually be uniform.

Functionally, the needle's eye should serve not only to carry threads through cloth or canvas, but to protect the thread from friction as it does so. Therefore, select needles with eyes large enough to prevent undue wear, but fine enough so that canvas and cloth will not be distorted by them.

For canvas, counted thread work, and loosely woven cloths, use tapestry needles. Their blunt points will not snag stitches or cloth. For other stitchery, pointed needles will be better; they are available in many sizes and types of eyes. Trial and error will find the best needle for a project, since so much of the choice is personal —it must be comfortable for your particular hand.

Frames: These are recommended. By holding canvas or cloth taut, not only can one-stroke stitching be done more easily but frames permit the use of both hands while working. This way, one hand remains on the surface of the work, the other under the frame, and needle and thread are transferred from one hand to the other, rather than moving a hand over the work to the back for each stroke.

Since canvas is starched, frames with rotating beams at top and bottom work well, and help prevent warping. They are available in several widths, are sometimes adjustable, and some have floor or table stands too.

For stitchery on cloth, an equalized tension is needed. There are square frames to which fabric can be tacked or lashed all around. There are also artists' canvas stretchers, which can be combined into many different sizes. These, too, can be used for canvas.

Perhaps the best-known frame for embroidery on cloth is the round or oval hoop, available in many sizes and several materials. These, too, can be had with floor or table stands of different types. Whichever type you choose, the outer hoop should have a screw adjustment, to accommodate different weights of cloth. In hoops, be sure the fabric is stretched on its grain; bias stretching will distort the embroidery.

Delicate base fabrics will require special treatment, as will areas already embroidered. For these, cut a strip or two of wrapping tissue the length of the hoop's circumference and about four times the width of the frame. Fold the strip over the inner hoop, and with masking tape or staples, fasten the loose sides together under the frame. Place cloth over the padded frame. Cover it with another sheet or two of tissue, fix the top hoop over all, then tear away tissue from working area.

Warning: Do not use hoops for canvas or counted thread work because of probable distortion of the stitch count.

Pattern Pencils: These are to be used with hot irons to transfer designs to cloth or canvas. The Joan Moshimer pencil is recommended since it will not bleed when wet while you are blocking or steaming the work.

Scissors: Have a sharp pair heavy enough to cut canvas and cloth, and a small, sharply pointed pair for snipping threads and removing stitches that do not please.

Seam Rippers: These can be helpful in removing unwanted stitches, but they are also dangerous. Use with caution; they can rip the base fabric along with the threads.

Thimbles: These surely save a fingertip. They should not bind the finger, nor be so loose they slip off; be sure the tip is smooth and will not snag threads and fabric.

Masking Tape: About 1½'' wide is a good size—it seems to stick to cut canvas edges better than the narrower tapes. This width is also more convenient for picking up lint from the actual needlework, nearby working surfaces, and your clothes, especially after raveling some stitches.

Paper Towels, Napkins: In hot or humid weather, hands do get grimy; wipe them frequently on these to keep embroidery and cloth more clean. Use also to polish needles.

Brass Polish: Grime adds up on needles, but a good brass polish helps to remove a lot of it.

ENLARGING DESIGNS

Diagrams for enlargement are surrounded by a scale of inch marks. Smaller spaces at either end of a scale represent fractions of inches, which will be included in the finished size of the design. The easiest, if somewhat costly, method of enlarging is a commercial mechanical photostat. In most urban areas there are several firms doing this kind of work. This way designs can be enlarged to any size, should those in the book not be convenient for you. Then, on heavy tracing paper, trace your stat with a hard pencil, and follow the transfer method described later (p. 7).

With some effort, an enlargement can be made by hand. Place a sheet of tracing paper over the book diagram; secure it to the page with small spring-type paper-clips—these do not mar the page. With a fineline marker and straight edge, draw lines connecting corresponding inch marks to form a grid over the diagram.

For the next step, graph paper with heavier inch marks will be most helpful. If sheets an inch or two larger than the actual design size are not available (at stationers or art suppliers), join smaller ones, matching the grid. Or, of course, you can draw your own grid, with lines 1'' apart, on a light-colored sheet of paper. Cover the grid with sturdy tracing paper, and staple together around the edges. With a hard pencil, draw the contents of each reduced square of the book grid to fill corresponding inch-size squares; do this one at a time until the entire design has been enlarged. Remove the drawing from the grid.

Should you desire a smaller or larger finished size than is in the book, draw the transfer grid to suit. If, for example, you want a 9'' design instead of a 12'' as shown, grid lines should be ¾'' apart, rather than 1''. On the other hand, a 1¼'' grid will produce a 15'' design.

If in the course of enlargement a circular outline is needed, the children's compasses available at variety stores will do them up to about 12'' in diameter. For larger circles, stick a pin through one end of a piece of string. Tie a pencil to the other end at desired radius. Hold pin at center of circle to be drawn. Then, keeping an even tension on the string, with the pencil perpendicular to the paper, draw circle all around the pin.

TRANSFERRING DESIGNS

For white or light-colored fabrics: Having made your enlargement, go over the drawing on the back side of the tracing paper with a hot-iron transfer pencil. Pin the drawing transfer, pencil side down, onto embroidery cloth or canvas. Horizontal and vertical lines should be along the grain of the cloth. Use a lot of pins, or baste the drawing to the cloth to keep it from moving. For the ironing, follow the directions that come with the pencil. Use a dry iron—steam will buckle the paper. Press and lift iron repeatedly over a spot—gliding it will produce double images. Be careful not to scorch paper, cloth, and especially canvas because of its starch. Be patient; work slowly to get clear impressions. Although it will slow down the process, cover the pencil enlargement with tissue paper to keep the soleplate of your iron clean.

If the base fabric is dark, a pattern pencil transfer might not be visible, but check this. There are at least two other methods that can be used. One is temporary fabric: Cotton or nylon organdie—or other sheers in white or light colors—is used for the actual transfer described above. Particularly if the organdie is cotton, press it between sheets of kitchen wax paper, and press it again between paper towels to remove excess wax.

Baste the transferred design to base cloth, checking that the grains of both fabrics match. Baste from the center out to each corner, to the top and bottom edges, and then out to each side. If needed, do some additional horizontal and vertical rows to keep the design from shifting. The embroidery is stitched through both fabrics, after which the sheer is cut and raveled away. The waxing makes this easier, as will eyebrow tweezers.

A second transfer method is to use dressmaker carbon in a light color. Place cloth on a hard surface, slip carbon, coated side down, between enlargement and cloth. Pin the enlargement to the base cloth as described in the hot-iron transfer. With a ballpoint pen, go over the drawing, making sure it has been transferred to the base.

Of course dark carbons can be used in the same way on light fabrics. But the iron-on seems to hold up better, and it will not smudge the cloth as carbon can.

BLOCKING

Unless the work has been done on a frame, most canvas embroidery will need blocking of some kind. For this each person has his or her own favorite method. Some recommendations follow.

Remove masking tape from the edges of the finished work carefully. Replace it with a narrow band of waterproof glue along the cut canvas edges. Tack a sheet of clear plastic to a wooden board, or homosote, which is several inches larger than the entire canvas. Smooth a bath towel over the plastic, tack it down at corners and at several places around the edges of the board. If the texture of the embroidery is smooth, tack it face down on the towel, in the unworked canvas margin, pulling it into square position. A box top is good for checking corner right angles should nothing else be available. Starting from the center of the top edge, and working out to each side, place tacks no more than ¾″ apart. In the same way pull sides into place, doing a few inches of each one at a time, all the way to the bottom edge. Then pull that straight. Canvas should be very taut.

Keep board flat throughout blocking process. Put a well-dampened towel over the stretched canvas. Cover that with another sheet of plastic until the dampness permeates the needlework. Then remove the plastic, but leave the damp towel in place until it and the embroidery are thoroughly dry—about four days if the weather is dry.

If the needlework is so warped it cannot be squared when dry, roll it in a damp towel and place in a plastic bag until the canvas is quite wet. Tack it to a toweled board as described above, keeping it wet the whole time with a clean sponge. Then cover it with a damp towel only and allow to dry flat.

Raised textures are treated in the same way, except that they are blocked face up.

Some needlework will require several blockings to straighten it, but it can be done.

PRESSING

For rumpled embroidery on cloth, pressing is usually enough of a finish. Spread a heavy bath towel on a board, and tack the embroidery face down around the edges of the cloth, pulling it smooth with care. Base cloths of cotton, linen, or wool can be steamed either with a steam iron and dry sheer cloth (to prevent snagging threads), or with a dry iron and damp cloth. Press lightly, never allowing the iron to rest on the stitching.

For work that is very soiled, some kind of cleaning will be needed before blocking and/or pressing. Crewel work (wool threads) might best be dry cleaned to avoid shrinkage. But do the pressing yourself since a light hand is needed. Cotton thread embroidery can be laundered with mild suds, then pressed while still damp as described above. Canvas work in wool can be laundered with mild suds or a cold-water detergent before pinning down for blocking. Be sure to glue the edges before laundering.

SOME GENERAL POINTS TO REMEMBER

All materials that come in contact with embroidery should be colorfast—markers and ballpoint pens must be permanent, and pins and tacks rustproof.

Protect all cut edges of fabric or canvas. For canvas, masking tape is good. Or bind with seam tape. For cloth, hand or machine overcasting will be adequate, since its edges are not likely to snag stitches or clothes or itself; even a narrow band of fabric glue will work.

Always buy more canvas or cloth than you expect to need. A larger project may be wanted midway through. Patching is unsightly, and even in canvas work, joining is unpleasant to do and not really invisible.

Mark "TOP" of embroidery or canvas on a strip of masking tape, so that you will always be aware of direction. If it will help, mark center space of canvas in each direction. Use a light gray (not black) fineline marker or basting thread. Sometimes counting from the center is easier than a long stretch across an edge. To find the centers of a piece, simply fold in half each way.

Count canvas threads with pins. Insert them after every 10th thread, checking each 10 before going on to the next. For total, count pins.

In any type of embroidery, do not float threads on the wrong side of work for more than ½''. They are usually pulled too taut, marring the surface appearance of the work, and they can be too easily snagged. Run threads from one place to another through the backs of stitches to maintain better tension and durability of the embroidery.

Never use knots in canvas embroidery; if possible, avoid them in all stitchery. Knots create wear and soil spots, and lumps on the face of the work. Hold starting thread ends in place on wrong side, to be caught in the first few stitches worked; or threads can be run through the backs of stitches before being brought to the surface.

Particularly for Basketweave and Continental work, end off threads by running them through the backs of stitches at an angle to the direction of stitching. This helps to avoid lumpy streaks.

Smoother embroidery, anyone? Where possible, do not bring the thread to the face of the work in a space (canvas) or hole (cloth) that already houses a stitch. This tends to ruffle or uproot the previous stitch.

For canvas work, bringing needle and thread to the surface in an empty space, and to the wrong side in a partly filled one, becomes a smoothing action for stitches that have already been worked. The same is true for stitchery on fabric.

When working with wools on canvas, fill in white and pale tones before brights and dark shades. In this way, lint from intense colors will not speckle pale tints.

If possible, do not completely surround an unfilled area of cloth or canvas with stitching. The center of the space will tend to mound, and not block or press out. Try to leave an opening in surrounding stitches until the area within has been worked.

If a canvas has been embroidered with Straight stitches, as in Bargello, outline the entire piece with about two rows of Continental stitch, in one of the medium-neutral shades in the work. A much better finish is achieved this way.

Basic
Stitches

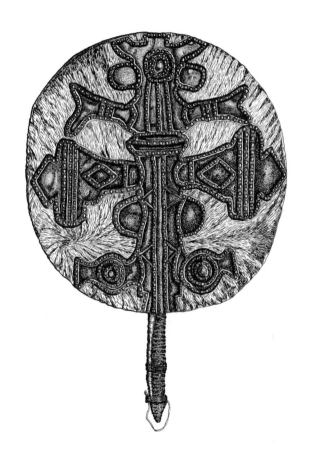

GOBELIN STITCHES

Upright Gobelin: These stitches are worked over any practical number of horizontal canvas threads, in spaces between the vertical threads. Done in horizontal rows, they imitate the ridged surface of Gobelin tapestries; the stitches in a single row are of the same height. Rows of Upright Gobelin can be worked either from right to left, or from left to right if more comfortable that way; but keep the same direction throughout the work by turning top edge to bottom for every second row. For all Gobelin stitches keep tension easy.

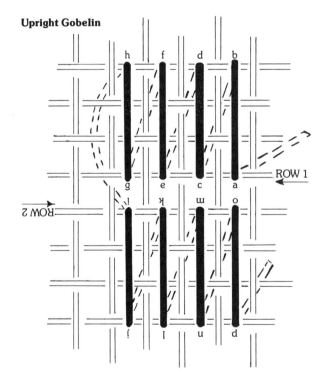

Upright Gobelin

Bargello

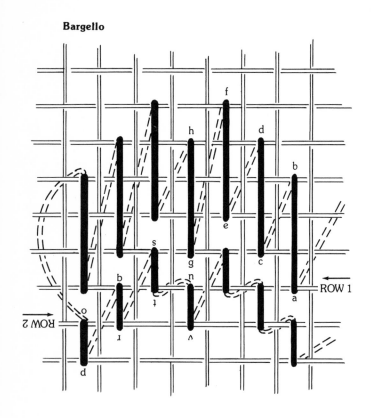

Bargello: The ascending and descending stitches of this technique—also known as Flame or Florentine stitch—are based on Upright Gobelin. They too can be of any practical height, which is usually constant within a single row. Work from right to left or left to right as you choose, but be consistent for most regular stitches. Turn canvas top edge to bottom for alternate rows.

To save wool, some needleworkers do their ascending stitches from bottom to top as shown in the diagram, and their descending stitches from the top of the work to the bottom. I prefer a constant direction of work to produce better-formed, more uniform stitches.

Horizontal Gobelin

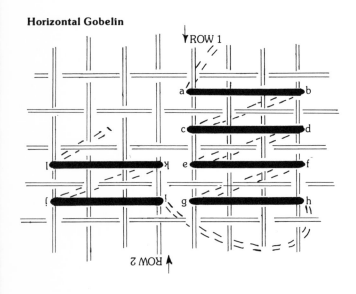

Horizontal Gobelin: Essentially the same in construction as Upright Gobelin, this variation is worked over vertical canvas threads to form vertical rows of stitches. It can be done from the top of a row downward, or upward from the bottom, as long as the direction of stitching remains the same. Therefore turn canvas top edge to bottom for every second row.

Oblique Gobelin, Wide Gobelin, Flat Filling Stitch: In this group of Gobelins, each one slants at a different angle. They are best worked from right to left, and with easy, even tension. To keep angles constant, turn work top edge to bottom for alternate rows.

Oblique Gobelin is stitched over any chosen number of horizontal canvas threads and crosses one vertical thread to the right.

Wide Gobelin is done the same way as Oblique. But it is a minimum of three horizontal threads of the canvas high and slants across two vertical threads.

Flat Filling stitch is worked at an angle of 45°—thus it crosses as many canvas threads in height as it does in width.

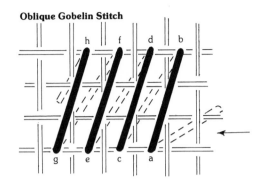

Oblique Gobelin Stitch

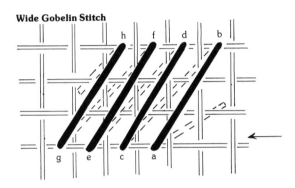

Wide Gobelin Stitch

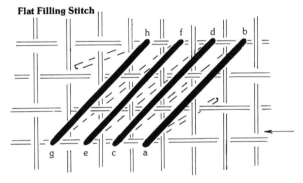

Flat Filling Stitch

MOSAIC, ALTERNATING MOSAIC, STITCHES

Basic Mosaic: Mosaic (a junior Scotch stitch really) is made up of three 45° stitches that form tiny square checks in canvas embroidery. Although it can be easily worked diagonally across the canvas or in vertical rows, it is shown here horizontally stitched. This way the canvas should be turned top edge to bottom for alternate rows, to keep the angle of the stitches constant.

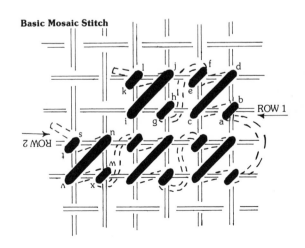

Basic Mosaic Stitch

Alternating Mosaic: In the finished work, the angle of the stitches changes every other check, the positions of each alternating at every row of checks. Although this too can be worked in either horizontal or vertical rows, when colors have also been alternated as in the Benin Leopard Spot on p. 68, a diagonal method of stitching is suggested; there will be no need to turn the canvas for this.

Start the SE/NW checks in the upper-left-hand corner, following the diagram. Be sure to skip the necessary four horizontal canvas threads as shown, to start Row 2 in an upward direction, at "g." Again skip four threads, this time vertical, to bring needle out at "y" for the beginning of downward Row 3. Continue in the same manner as for Rows 2 and 3.

Assuming, for illustration purposes only, that there will be a multiple of four canvas threads across the design, SW/NE rows would start in the upper-right-hand corner of the canvas; these threads would not have been filled by the previous rows of checks. The diagram shows the start of the first check at "a." Except for reversing the direction of stitches, the construction is the same virtually as before. The complete pattern stitch is shown below.

Alternating Mosaic Stitch

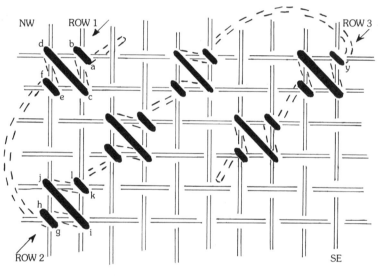

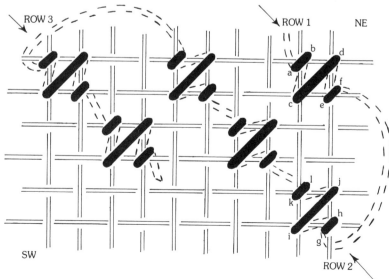

Completed Alternating Mosaic Stitch

BASKETWEAVE, CONTINENTAL STITCHES

More formally known as Tent stitches, these look-alikes are probably the most frequently used for canvas embroidery. In each of the constructions, a stitch diagonally covers a canvas mesh; after the first stitch, two canvas threads are skipped on the wrong side before working the next stitch. Basketweave is stitched diagonally across the canvas; Continental is done in horizontal or vertical rows to cover an area.

Basketweave: Although Continental can always be substituted for Basketweave, the latter has advantages for which its use is highly recommended. The canvas need not be turned for alternate rows; it will not be as warped when stitched in this way. The wrong side of the canvas, resembling a basketweave—hence its name—is more evenly covered and padded, giving greater loft to the finished work.

The expanded diagram for Basketweave shows that after a first stitch (in a corner here), there follow, in alphabetical steps, alternate downward and upward rows to fill in a space. Though the direction of stitching is always SE/NW, almost any shape can be worked. However, unless there is a change of color, do not work two consecutive "up" or "down" rows, since it will cause streaking. To avoid this, check the wrong side of the canvas for the last row worked. The diagram shows that "up" rows form horizontal floats on the canvas back, as from "h" to "j" and "k" to "l," while downward rows leave vertical floats, like "d−e" in Row 2 and those of Row 4. Basketweave will do one-stitch-wide rows only if they are at the angle of its construction. For others, Continental must be used.

Basketweave Stitch

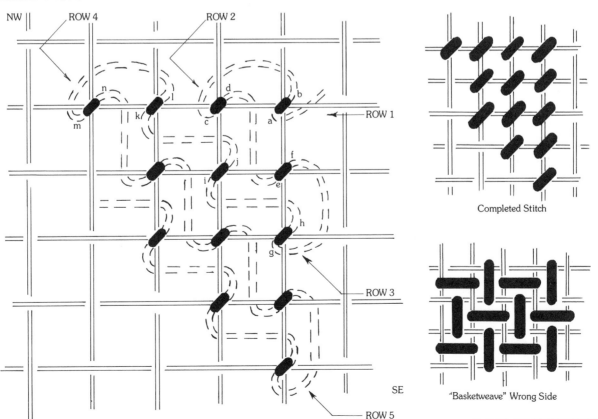

Completed Stitch

"Basketweave" Wrong Side

Continental: The diagram of this construction, expanded alphabetically, shows its simplicity. Canvas must, however, be turned top edge to bottom for alternate rows. Unless a frame and two-handed method of stitching is used, the canvas will be very warped. The stitch is more difficult to work on double-mesh canvas than Basketweave. There will be places where Continental must be used—for one-stitch lines, horizontal, vertical, and NE/SW diagonals.

Continental Stitch

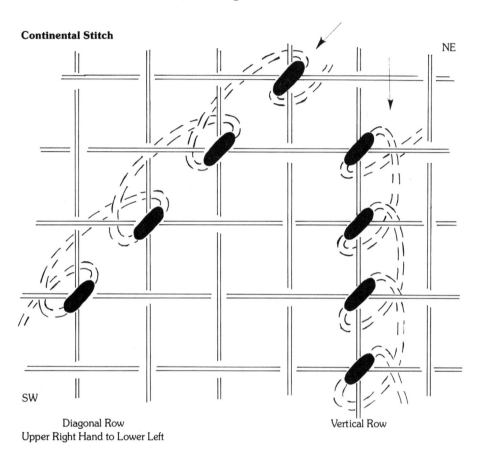

NE

SW

Diagonal Row
Upper Right Hand to Lower Left

Vertical Row

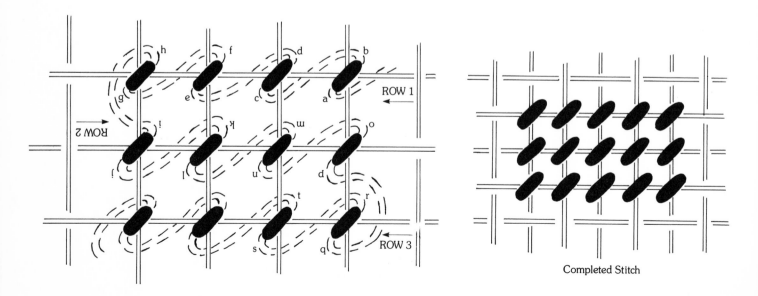

Completed Stitch

INTERWOVEN STITCH

This combination of Upright and Horizontal Gobelin can be worked in horizontal or vertical rows. The neatest, most pleasant, and economical way, however, is diagonally across the canvas, resembling the more familiar Basketweave. When doing the stitch this way, the canvas need not be turned. Horizontal blocks are done in a downward NW/SE direction; vertical blocks are worked upward.

Interwoven is usually embroidered in blocks of three stitches worked over four canvas threads as shown, but almost any size block looks good. However, there must always be one stitch less in each block than the number of canvas threads covered by each stitch.

Interwoven Stitch

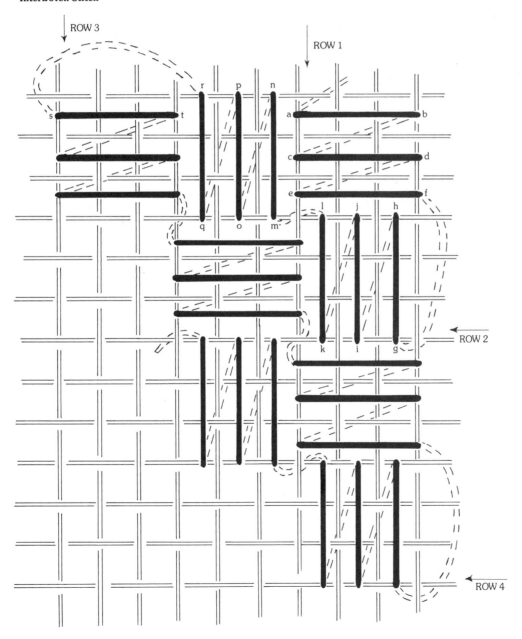

CHAIN STITCH

Decorative and versatile, the Chain stitch is used for fillings, heavier outlines, and for padding under stitches such as Satin. Among its many variations are Zigzag, Twisted, Open, Broad, and Knotted. It can be done on canvas, or on fabric as shown here in the schematic diagram.

For most hands, working from a generally right-hand direction toward the left or from the top to the bottom of a stitching line—indicated by dashes through the center of the schematic—is more comfortable. Dotted lines represent the movement of the working thread on the wrong side.

Thread is brought to the face of the cloth at point "a." Circle thread counterclockwise back to "a," forming an ample loop. As the loop is held in place with the left thumb, working thread goes to the wrong side again at "a," and under the cloth to emerge at "b"—the desired length of Chain stitch link. Bring thread over the held-down loop. Now draw working thread out until loop fits against it at "b." For best-looking links, do not pull taut. Again swing thread up, left, and back around to "b." As for the first link, take stitch from "b" to "c" on wrong side, bringing thread out and over loop. Complete link as before and continue in this way for desired length of chain. To end a chain, bring thread to the wrong side just to the left of the last-formed link—see completed stitch diagram.

When used for filling, keeping the same direction of stitching within an area will produce a smoother surface; give the chains enough room to spread a little between rows. Be especially careful to maintain an easy tension when working from the outside line toward the center of a motif. This will prevent mounding or bulging in the mid-section of each unit.

Chain Stitch

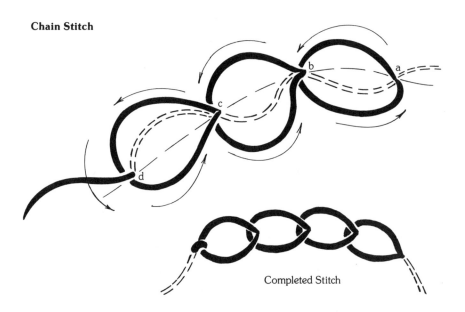

Completed Stitch

OUTLINE AND STEM STITCH

Both of these stitches are worked from the left hand toward the right, or from the bottom toward the top. Their difference is in the position of the working thread during the stitching. Stem stitch is done with the thread held toward the right or below the needle as each new stitch is taken; for Outline stitch, the thread is to the left of the needle or above it. In either case, a ropy look results; if a row of Stem stitch is done close to and on the right side of a row of Outline, a chained effect results.

Profile schematics for classic Outline and Stem stitches are shown in the diagram, as well as the finished appearance of each. The dashes represent stitching lines; dotted lines indicate the course of the working thread on the wrong side. Follow the stitching sequences in alphabetical order, drawing threads close to the fabric with each step.

Each of the stitches can be made more compact by reducing the amount of space between points "b" and "e," and "d" and "f," or closing it completely. Also, as shown in the bottom diagram, a row of stitches can be made slightly wider by taking each new stitch at a slight angle across the stitching line.

Closely worked rows of either stitch make a rich filling texture; for the smoothest effect, keep rows all in the same stitching direction.

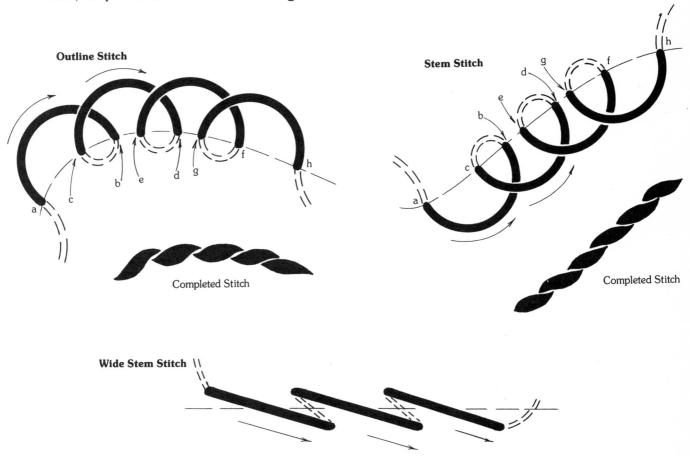

Outline Stitch

Completed Stitch

Stem Stitch

Completed Stitch

Wide Stem Stitch

BUTTONHOLE (BLANKET) STITCH

Used to finish an edge (cut or folded), or for filling and decoration, the variations of this stitch are uncountable. Its vertical stitches can be grouped in clusters of two or more and widely spaced, or they can be graduated in length, angled to converge, or slanted in one direction. Two rows of Buttonhole stitch can be turned so that the vertical stitches of one nest in the spaces between the verticals of the other. There are knotted varieties, and the very important Tailor's Buttonhole stitch. "Blanket" usually implies that there is some space between each of the vertical stitches; Buttonhole itself is so closely worked that no base fabric is visible. Their construction however, is identical. Although the more usual left-hand to right-hand direction of work is shown, some hands may find working from the right more comfortable; for this, hold diagram in front of a mirror to reverse it.

Two parallel stitching lines are needed for Buttonhole stitch. The thread comes through the fabric at a point on the lower line. Keeping left thumb on working thread, loop it around toward the right, take a stitch under the fabric from "b" on the upper line to "c" directly below it on the lower line. Bring working thread over the loop, then draw it out until a vertical bar is formed and held in place by the working thread. Place left thumb on this intersection of threads, then in the same way work the desired number of stitches.

The lower diagram shows completed stitches. To end a row, take working thread to the wrong side just to the right of the last vertical at "f" on the lower stitching line.

Buttonhole (Blanket) Stitch

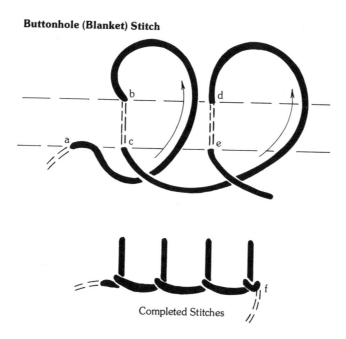

Completed Stitches

HERRINGBONE STITCH

In both dressmaking and embroidery, Herringbone stitch is decorative and functional. It can also be used on canvas.

The stitch is done between two stitching lines—the dashes on the diagram—and from the left hand toward the right. Dotted lines represent working thread on the wrong side of the cloth, though when fully drawn, it will look like rows of Running stitch. Follow the alphabetical stitching order in the diagram. Note that upper crossings of threads are centered between the lower. Despite this, the stitch can be worked around curves. If stitches are long, watch your tension carefully so that they will not gather up the base cloth.

Close(d) Herringbone is the same stitch worked so that stitch end "g" will be at point "b," "i" will be at "d," "k" at "f," "m" at "h," and so on.

Herringbone stitch is also used for shadow work on sheer fabrics—the reverse of the stitch will then be on the right side of the cloth.

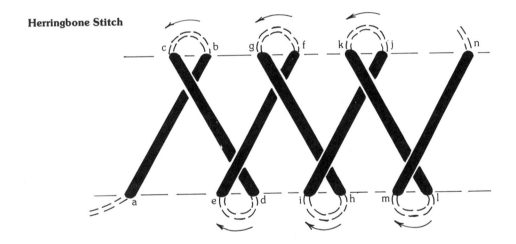

Herringbone Stitch

SCOTCH STITCH

Like Mosaic, Scotch stitch forms a checked ground; unlike Mosaic, these checks are composed of at least five diagonal stitches, shown on the diagram, which can alternate every block if desired. Scotch stitch can be easily done in horizontal or vertical rows. And since the pleasant diagonal method shown does not require turning canvas for alternate rows, it is a boon when covering large areas. As in Basketweave, do not stitch two consecutive upward or downward rows; a slightly different pull on the backs of stitches may cause slight streaking.

Each stitch within a check diagonally covers as many canvas threads in width as it does in height; for larger checks, increase the number of threads covered up to a center stitch, then decrease the lengths of stitches to correspond.

A ground can be started by working an "up" check (in alphabetical order) from "a" through "j." A "down" row starts at "k" and continues out to the right-hand edge. Note that each check is in line with the previous ones. Dotted lines show the course of the working thread between stitches and checks on the wrong side of the canvas.

Scotch Stitch

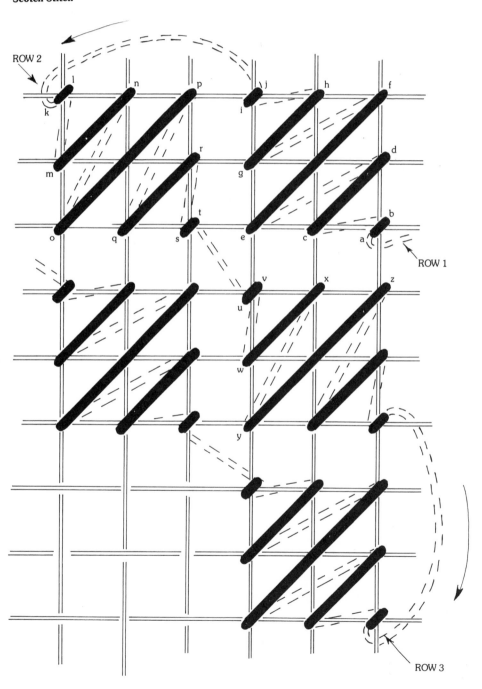

CROSS STITCH

For counted thread embroidery on cloth or canvas, Cross stitch has long been a standby; its uses and variations are legion. The working method on canvas will depend on its type, or on the height and width of the stitches, which can be equal, oblong, or wide. But regardless of method, one rule *must* be followed: All top crossing stitches must be in the same direction. Here, top crossovers are shown from SW to NE.

Two-journey crosses are probably more pleasant to stitch; also, they help to keep the direction of top crossing the same. On double-mesh canvas, any size Cross stitch can be worked in this way. On mono, however, stitches must be two or more canvas threads high and wide to be done this way. SE/NW understitches in the diagram make up the first journey, which starts from the right-hand side—"a−b," "c−d," and "e−f." For the return journey, the working thread is brought down for stitches from "g" to "h," "i−j," and "k−l." Note the vertical threads between each Cross stitch (dotted lines on the diagram) on the wrong side of the work.

A single-journey method is needed on mono canvas when Cross stitches are worked over one canvas mesh only, or when only one Cross stitch is wanted. That is, each Cross stitch must be complete before the next is begun. For clarity

Cross Stitch

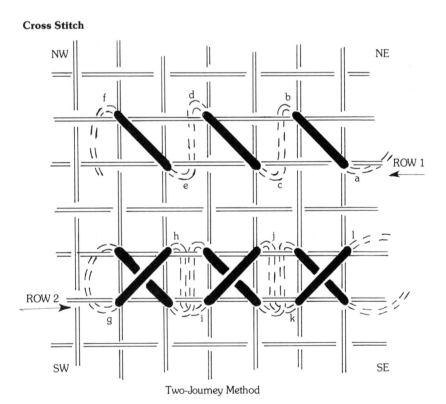

Two-Journey Method

only, this method is also shown worked over two canvas threads in height and width. In alphabetical order from the right, understitch "a−b" is crossed by "c−d." The working thread is then carried down and across for "e−f," which is then crossed by "g−h." Continue in this way for desired number of stitches.

A vertical row of Cross stitches from the top downward is done in a similar manner. Starting from the right hand, understitch "a−b" is crossed by "c−d"; then the working thread swoops down for next understitch "e−f," which is crossed by "g−h."

A diagonal row of Cross stitches is also done single journey.

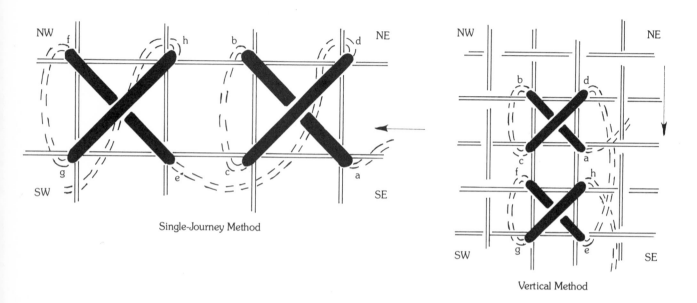

Single-Journey Method

Vertical Method

UPRIGHT CROSS STITCH

Although the diagram shows alternate methods of working this filling stitch, the diagonal is preferred; crossings of vertical and horizontal stitches are more nearly perpendicular when done this way, and the wrong side is less confused. Vertical stitches are worked from the lower right hand diagonally upward toward the left. Horizontals are stitched from the left hand in a downward diagonal toward the right. The construction can be started with a first Upright Cross in the upper-right-hand corner. Vertical stitch "a−b" is followed by fill-in "c−d." Working down now, horizontal "e−f" completes the cross, then fill-in "g−h" completes the row. Following the diagram in alphabetical order, Row 3 starts with vertical "i−j" for the next set of Upright Crosses, which will be completed on Row 4.

These stitches have been "worked" over two canvas threads in each direction, but any desired even number of canvas threads can be used; crossed stitches are centered between those of the previous row. It can also be done on even-weave cloth. Be sure to use heavy enough wool or thread to cover the grounds completely if larger stitches are used. If horizontal rows of complete crosses are worked, turn canvas top edge to bottom on alternate rows for better results. It should be obvious that if you wish, your topmost stitch of the crosses can be vertical.

Upright Cross Stitch

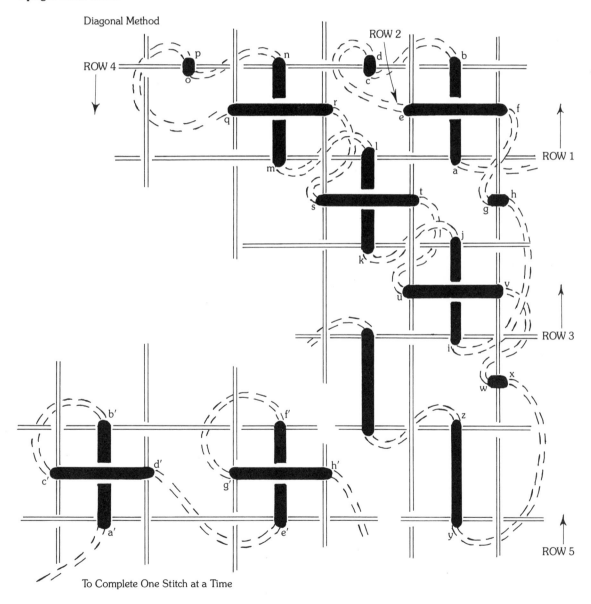

Diagonal Method

To Complete One Stitch at a Time

BRICK STITCH

Brick stitch can be used for both canvas and embroidery cloths, particularly the even weaves. Here it is shown on canvas worked over four threads, though it can be done over any even number from two on up; on alternate rows stitches lie halfway between those of the previous row.

To establish "brick" formation, a first row of long and short stitches is worked. After that, stitches will be of even length except for final row, which will be similar to the first. Turn canvas top edge to bottom on second and all even rows to keep

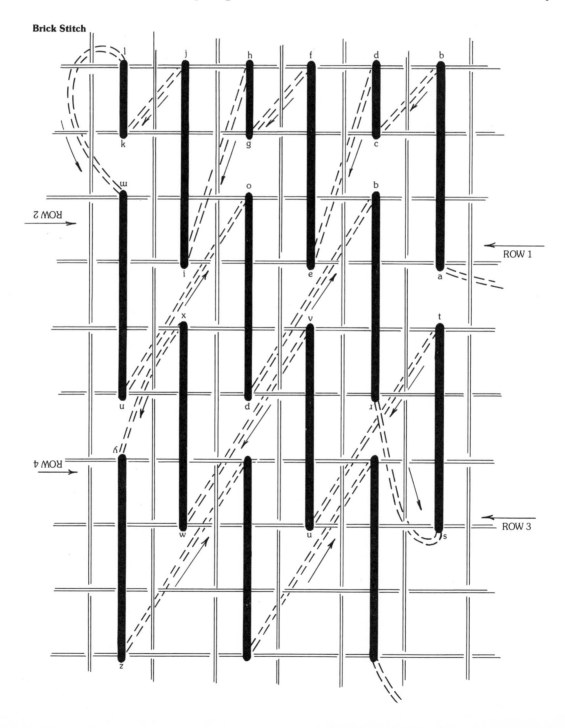

Brick Stitch

stitches parallel. And, as a further precaution, working only alternate stitches on each row as shown will "pull" them at the same angle on the wrong side of the work. Follow diagram alphabetically. Especially for upright stitches, use only enough tension to control; do not pull working thread taut.

LAZY DAISY STITCH

Also known as plain Daisy and Detached Chain, the latter is exactly what the stitch is. Though largely used for petal shapes and leaves, when regularly spaced, spattered, or freely layered it can be a worthwhile filling texture.

The schematic diagram shows the stitch worked radially between two stitching lines—the dashes. Dotted lines represent the course of the working thread on wrong side of the cloth. Though the construction is shown worked counterclockwise and from bottom to top, you can use any direction that is comfortable.

Bring working thread to the face of the fabric at "a" on lower stitching line. In either direction—but be consistent—loop it upward and back around to "a." There, take thread to wrong side for long stitch to "b" on the upper line and inside the loop, which should be held with the left thumb. Draw working thread out and over the loop, until loop fits against it at "b"; tie loop down with small stitch "b–c." Without pulling thread taut, bring it to the face of fabric again on lower line at point "d" for next Daisy loop. Continue in this manner. For well-rounded Daisy stitches, keep tension easy; for more oval loops, draw thread a little more taut.

Lazy Daisy Stitch

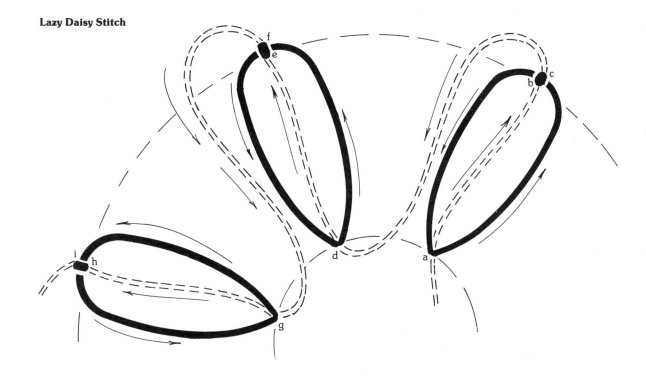

BYZANTINE STITCH

This interesting canvas-filling stitch is nicely textured and covers large areas quickly. Its 45° stitches can be worked over any practical number of canvas threads. The height of stitches must be the same as their width. Although the steps of this pattern must also be as wide as they are high, almost any number of stitches within them will be effective.

For convenience in diagrammatic form, the stitches shown here are three canvas threads high by three threads wide; three stitches lie between the angle-pivot stitches "e−f," "m−n," "e'−f'", and so on. Dotted lines represent the working wool on wrong side of the canvas; thus the order of stitching can be followed. Turn canvas top edge to botton for second and all even rows to keep the stitch angle uniform. And keep tension easy.

Note that angle-pivot stitches form a SW/NE diagonal line across the canvas, and that steps always nest into each other.

STRAIGHT STITCHES

As their name implies, these are random detached stitches of varied lengths and directions. The only working problem is being careful not to pull threads taut between stitches on the wrong side.

For well-formed stitches, be consistent in their construction. If possible, always work from either the bottom of a stitch to its top, or the top to the bottom—not both. The stitching order is shown alphabetically; dotted lines indicate the course of thread on wrong side of work. In this type of stitch, you can work from right to left, or left to right, or both.

Straight Stitches

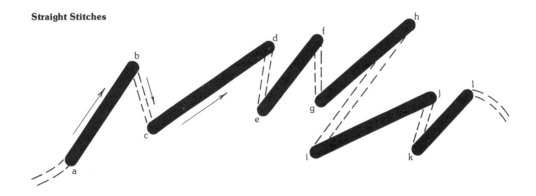

Byzantine Stitch

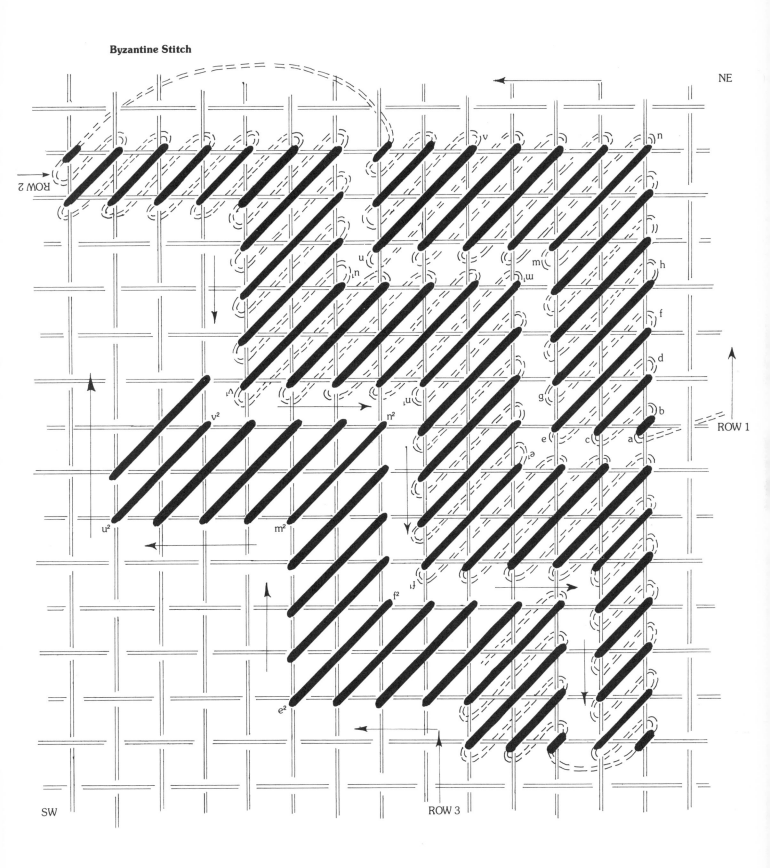

NE

ROW 2

SW

ROW 3

ROW 1

FLY STITCH

On cloth, this is a pleasant filling and decorative stitch. It can be worked around curves, or radially, evenly spotted across an area, or stitched so closely it looks like Satin stitch with a center accent.

Bring working thread to surface at point "a" on the left-hand stitching line—dashes on either side of the stitch. Form a semicircular loop downward and toward the right. At "b" on the right-hand stitching line, take thread to wrong side and diagonally down and over to "c"—the desired depth of stitch. It emerges for tie-down stitch "c–d" at midpoint and over the loop. Dotted lines show the course of thread on wrong side of work.

For next stitch, thread comes up again at "e" on left-hand line, loops around to "f" on right-hand line, and is completed as before with tie-down "g–h" over the loop.

Either direction of looping will work; but do be consistent for better-formed stitches. Do not pull working thread taut between stitches.

Fly Stitch

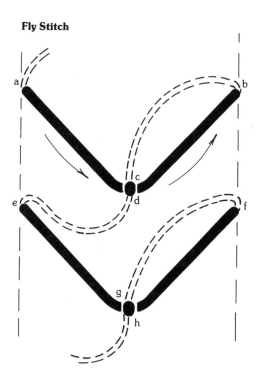

SATIN STITCH

Most people know its name and lustrous smoothness, but practiced embroiderers realize that Satin stitch is one of the more difficult to do well. Done on fabrics, it should have the look of woven satin, and except for encroaching stitches, it should show clean, sharp edges. Stitches can be of any practical length, at any angle, and to any contour; but they should be parallel and close.

Satin stitch construction is simple, resembling the overhand motion of Upright Gobelin. In the top diagram, working thread is brought to the face of the cloth at "a," back to the wrong side at "b." At "c," as close as possible to "a," the thread comes to the surface again; it is taken to the wrong side at "d," as close as possible to "b," and so on.

On the right-hand end of the diagram, working thread emerges at "k" for the last stitch—dotted lines show the course of the thread on wrong side; that stitch would be completed at "l." Dashes represent stitching lines for top and bottom ends of stitches.

The center drawing shows Satin stitch worked at an angle.

If fine, soft threads are being used, padding under the Satin stitch will help its appearance. This understitching can be of Running (as in sewing), Split, or Chain stitches, worked perpendicular to the Satin. When shapes must be well defined, also Run-stitch around the edges before covering with Satin.

If a project is to be a wall hanging, stitch lengths are of no concern. However, an article subject to wear should be done with shorter stitches. Particularly for long stitches, be careful not to pull them taut so as to avoid puckering the fabric.

Encroaching Satin Stitch: When a more blended edge between rows of Satin stitch is required, stitches of one row can be "encroached" between those of a previous row. This means that the top ends of a new stitch row are forced between the lower ends of the row before it, so that they overlap slightly. The saw-toothed line that results is particularly effective when a different tone of color is used in each row. Encroaching stitches can be worked at any angle.

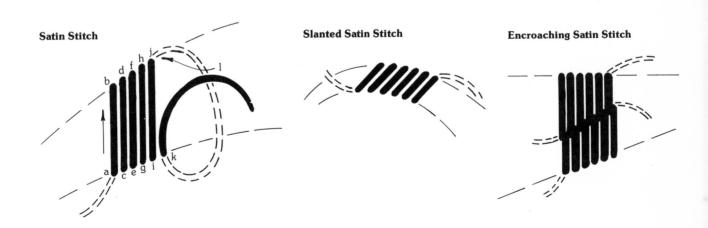

Satin Stitch   **Slanted Satin Stitch**   **Encroaching Satin Stitch**

SPLIT STITCH

For this construction, a softly twisted thread or wool, or ideally an even number of threads per working strand, is needed. Each new stitch divides (splits) the thread(s) of a previous one. Because of this, the completed work resembles fine Chain stitching, and can be used for fillings or outlines on cloth in the same way. In the diagram, dashes represent the stitching line, dots show end of a stitch covered by next stitch, and short dashes indicate the course of working thread on wrong side of cloth.

Work in a generally left to right or bottom-upward direction, as for Stem stitch. Bring thread to face of cloth on stitching line for beginning stitch "a," then back to the wrong side at its desired length. For stitch "b," working thread again comes to the surface through the center of "a" thread at about one-quarter of its length from the end; stitches should be of equal length. Complete "b" as for "a." Working thread again splits thread(s) of "b" stitch for beginning of stitch "c"; continue in this way. The diagram shows working thread dividing stitch "d" to start the next.

For fillings, the texture is soft and diffused. Work consecutive rows only close enough to cover the base fabric; allow space for splitting to spread the thread of the stitches. Stitching in the same direction will make for smoother texture than if rows are turned alternately. If the frame method of embroidery—two-handed—is used, then the stitch will be flat on the cloth when split. However, if stitches are worked in one stroke, the thread to be split will be slightly up in the air.

Split Stitch

Gold Coast Kente.
See page 119.

Kente Cloth.
See page 129.

Ibo Applique.
See page 134.

Fon Applique.
See page 132.

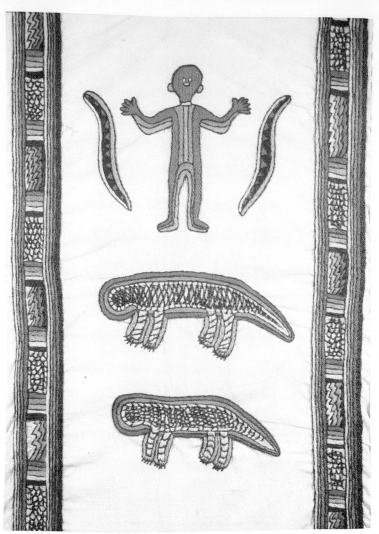

Liberian Hunter.
See page 122.

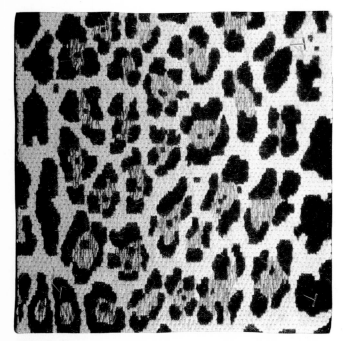

Cheetah Skin.
See page 96.

Lesotho Leaf.
See page 86.

Chief's Fan.
See page 88.

Olokun Adire.
See page 116.

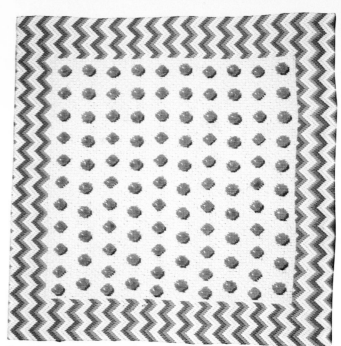

Benin Leopard.
See page 66.

Benin Leopard Spot. See page 68.

Bronze Rooster.
See page 64.

Benin Head.
See page 46.

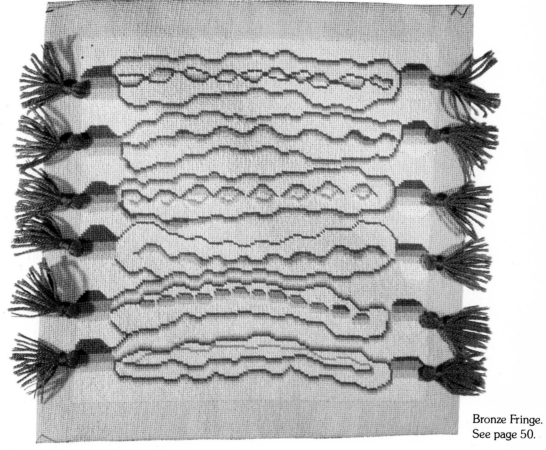

Bronze Fringe.
See page 50.

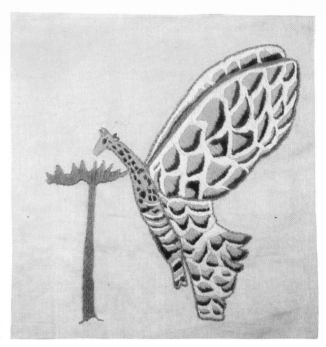

Ornithoptera Girafficus.
See page 92.

Akan Quilt. See page 98.

Nigerian Beaded Bag.
See page 76.

Burlap Fishscales.
See page 59.

Burlap Fish—Wall Hanging.
See page 58.

Nigerian Puff.
See page 70.

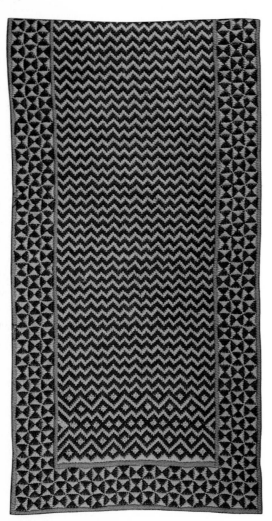

Zaire Bark Fabric (Runner).
See page 113.

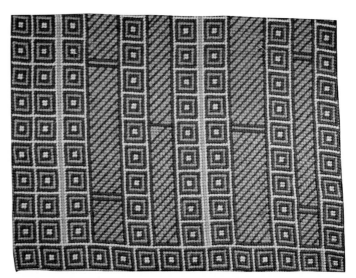

Lagos Rug.
See page 80.

COUCHING

Couched (tied-down) threads produce interesting textures for outlines and fillings, since threads of different weights and colors can be effectively used at one time. And it is pleasant and uncomplicated to work. If different thicknesses of threads are to be used, the couched (laid) strand is usually heavier than the, couching (tie-down) thread.

At "a" on the stitching line—shown by dashes in the diagram—bring thread to be laid to face of cloth, float it along the stitching line, then take it to the wrong side at "b"; do not fasten, but keep ends free for adjusting tension during the couching. Work in any comfortable direction, but be consistent; keep space between tie-downs even and their angle the same. Dotted lines show the course of threads on the wrong side.

Couching thread now comes to the surface at point "c," a short distance from "a," and below laid strand. With close, firm stitches ("c—d," "e—f," "g—h," etc.) tack "a—b" in place, ending a short space before "b." Be careful not to pull couching thread taut between stitches. With thinner or couching thread, fasten the laid strand on the wrong side; trim, leaving short ends beyond fastening.

Couching

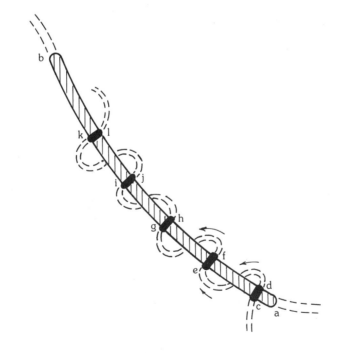

DARNED FILLING—DIAGONAL

This construction will pose no problem for those who have darned socks. The difference here is that the darning is interwoven diagonally, and there is no hole to cover. This darning is worked on the surface of cloth. For best results, use a frame to keep cloth taut. The spacing of threads is optional, but must be even; the angle of darning is optional too, as long as opposite diagonals are the same.

In the left-hand diagram, working thread comes to the face of the cloth at "a," floats in SE direction to "b," where it returns to the wrong side for short stitch "b—c." From "c," lay thread diagonally toward NW to "d" for another wrong-side stitch "d—e." Dotted lines show the course of thread on wrong side of work. Continue in this manner until space to be covered is filled.

Now, as shown in the right-hand block, thread is carried on the wrong side from "r" of the last float to emerge at "s" for darning in an opposite SW/NE direction. Do not pick up any base cloth except for connecting stitches on the wrong side. A tapestry needle will make darning easier.

From "s," working thread goes under float "m—n," over "k—l," then to wrong-side stitch "t—u." On face of work again, take thread over "j—i," under "k—l," over "m—n," under "o—p," then to wrong side for stitch "v—w." Continue in this manner until all floats have been crossed and "woven." Easy tension is a must for fillings of this sort. Naturally, Darned Filling can also be done on the square as for socks.

Darned Filling—Diagonal

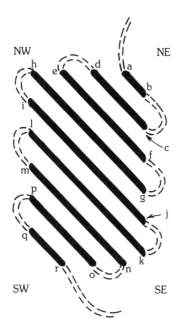

LAID FILLINGS—COUCHED

A frame should be used for this work, to prevent puckering the base cloth. As in Darned Filling, cross threads are laid over an area; but instead of being interwoven, they are held to the base cloth with small tie-down stitches as in couching. This can be done with the same or thinner threads.

For square filling, evenly spaced horizontal and vertical threads are laid across the area—no matter which is done first. In the diagram, dotted lines show the course of the working threads on the wrong side. Thread comes to the face of the fabric at "a" and is drawn upward to "b." Take stitch "b−c" on wrong side, then float thread "c−d" in a downward direction. Continue to follow the diagram alphabetically until all vertical threads are on. Do not pull them taut. In the same way float horizontal threads "k−l," "m−n," "o−p," and so on over the verticals. At the intersections of these threads, take small Half-Cross stitches (in either direction) to fasten the laid threads to the cloth. Turn work top edge to bottom for alternate rows; or if full Cross stitches are used as tie-downs, work two journeys and do not turn cloth.

Laid Fillings—Couched Square

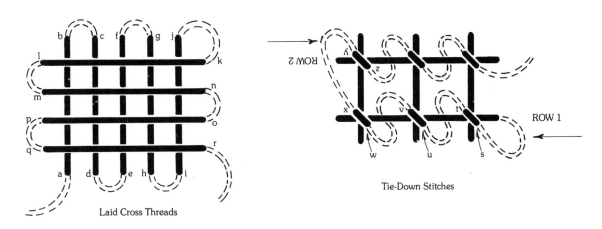

Laid Cross Threads

Tie-Down Stitches

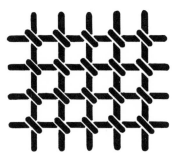

Completed Filling

Diagonal Filling is done in a similar way. Again keep threads evenly spaced and keep opposite diagonals at the same angle. In the diagram, SW/NE diagonal threads "a−b" through "k−l" are laid on first. These are topped with SE/NW floats "m−n" through "w−x." In this case, tie-downs at intersections can be either vertical, as shown in alphabetical order, or horizontal, or both. For this last, *see* Upright Cross stitch, p. 26. If only one of the tie-downs is used, turn work for alternate rows to keep stitches more parallel.

Laid Fillings—Couched Diagonal

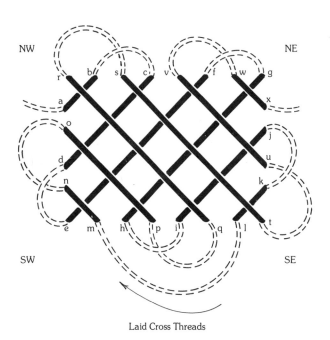

Laid Cross Threads

Tie-Down Stitches

FRENCH KNOTS

Since these are little more than overhand knots stitched into fabric, it is surprising that some needleworkers are troubled by them.

For practice, stretch some cloth on a frame. If possible, use a needle that is more straight than tapered, and with a long eye. Again for practice, use fairly heavy yarn or thread. Bring the thread to the face of the fabric through point "a" on a stitching line; from there, swing the working thread in a counterclockwise loop as shown in diagram Step 1. Place left thumb on loop to the left of "a," or hold it between thumb and forefinger. This should not be a death grip, but a controlling force; the working thread must be eased with the movements of the needle. From above, slide the point of the needle under the thread at "a," then—Step 2—lift it slightly so that thread rests on its point. Still restraining loop with left thumb, pivot needle in a small, clockwise arc to insert its point in "b"—a fabric thread or so from "a." This motion will cause working thread to be wrapped around the needle.

Now take needle to the wrong side, drawing working thread through. As it shortens and nears the knot, very slightly relax the thumb hold until the knot is fully closed.

There are three major reasons for problems when working with French Knots. The first is too thick a needle for the thread being used; the second is wrapping thread around the needle so tightly that the resulting twist is pulled to the wrong side with the needle; and the third is not skipping fabric threads between points "a" and "b."

If a heavier knot is desired, use heavier or more strands of thread, rather than twisting thread around the needle more than once. French Knots can be worked closely as a filling or spattered over a wider area.

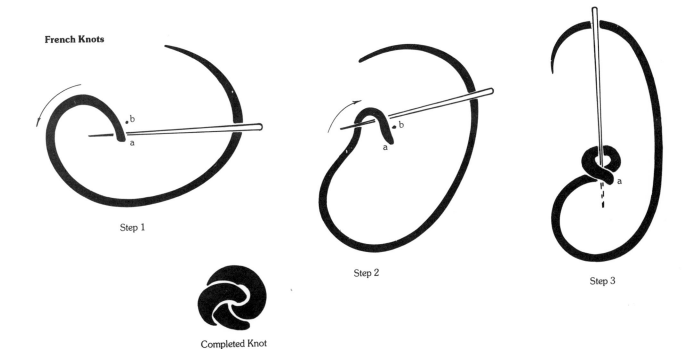

French Knots

Step 1

Step 2

Step 3

Completed Knot

The Projects

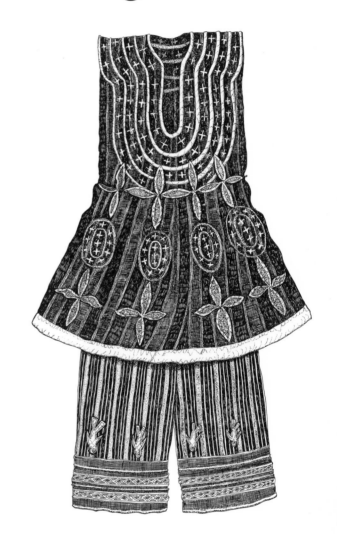

AFRICAN MAP

A review of many early African maps inspired this design, with its embroidery in the "missionary style."

Size: Outside diameter is about 24″; the starry border is about 1″ wide

Materials: White handkerchief linen or similar-quality cotton, skipper blue linen or cotton of the same weight and texture, about 25″ square; six-strand embroidery cotton, using two threads at a time; sewing thread to match the blue fabric.

For those who like the tiny stitches of fine embroidery, this map will be a happy project. Start with the "geographical" detail within the continent. Stem-stitch desert sands with sand (A). Palm tree trunks are Split-stitched, the foliage is in Stem stitch with small Lazy Daisy loops hanging from the lowest branches—all in apple green (C). Behind the palms is taupe (D) Buttonhole stitch. Bodies of the gazelle, camel, and giraffe are worked in camel (B) Split stitch. Gazelle antlers are Satin stitch, its legs Straight stitches couched down at knee joints. For all wildlife, any dark color will do for a tiny eye stitch. The giraffe's legs are like the gazelle's, but the camel's are done in Satin stitch.

In each of the foliage sprays, larger leaves are sap green (F) Satin stitch, stems are Stem stitch; the smaller leaves are C Satin stitch. There is a small F Lazy Daisy flower on the lower spray. Work the crocodile in F Satin stitch, diverging from the center of the beast. Both elephant and rhino are done in D Split stitch. The bird is palest yellow H Split stitch. Mounds around the southern portion of the continent are Split stitch in F and D. Work the branches in wheat (E) Stem stitch. Stem-stitch the Nile and other rivers with gray (J), the lakes with pale blue (G). Also Stem-stitch the inside outline of the continent with J, the outer boundary with medium blue (K).

"Africa," too, is K, but Satin stitch. Malagasy Island in J and K is outlined like Africa itself.

In the northeastern part of the hemisphere, outline the sun symbol face with B Stem stitch. Eyebrows and mouth are B Satin stitch, but nose and eyes are Stem stitch. The sun's rays are couched alternately with H and yellow (M).

Next, stitch in the oceans around the continent. First, with foam white (L), French-Knot the centers (dots) of the billows. To avoid mounding the base cloth, be most careful about tension when Stem-stitching spiral and concentric "waves." Note that the seas around Malagasy are G, but the remaining waters are done in a deeper but still light blue (I).

Now prepare the border. On the square of blue fabirc, draw concentric circles, the diameters of inside and outside border edges. Then draw in seam allowance at least ⅜'' on each side of the circular blue band. Cut out the band on seam allowance lines, being careful not to stretch the edges.

Baste the band in place around the map so that the seam allowance overlaps the stitching. Turn under the allowance all around on each edge of the band; slash or notch it as needed so that the band will lie flat; baste the edges down. Very neatly hem the band in place.

With L, embroider "stars" at irregular intervals all around the blue band. These are simply Straight stitches, which first form an "X"; a thin stitch crosses the center of the X.

Opposite:
Early African map
embroidered in
"missionary" style

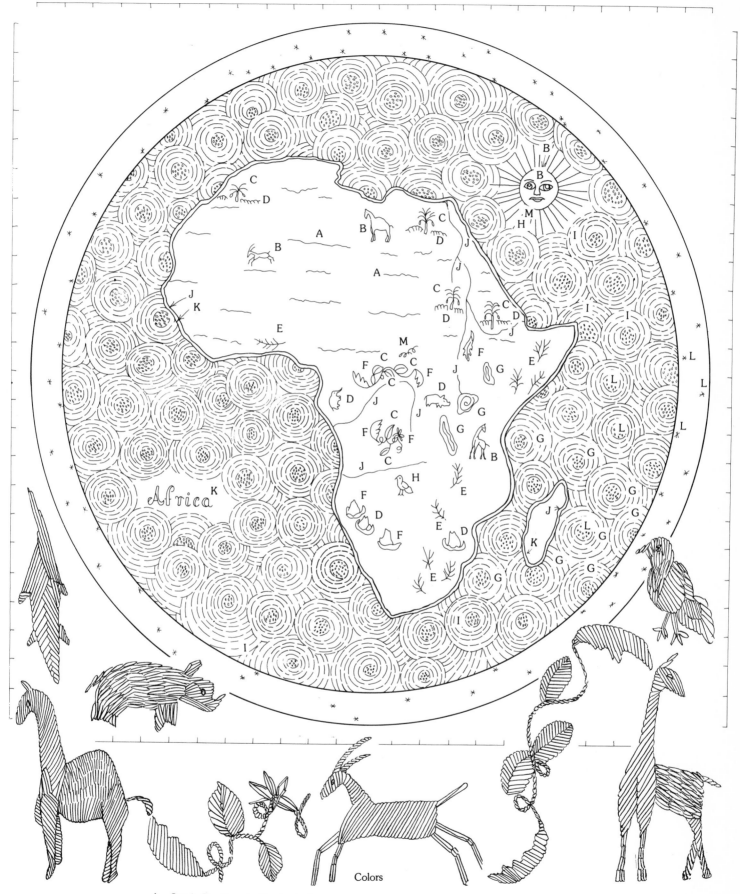

Colors

A—Sand B—Camel C—Apple Green D—Taupe E—Wheat F—Sap Green G—Pale Blue

H—Palest Yellow I—Light Blue J—Gray K—Medium Blue L—Foam White M—Yellow

Drawing of the head of a
Benin king in bronze. Nigeria.
American Museum of Natural History

BENIN HEAD

*This portrait head of a Benin king is cast in bronze. Many other portrait heads
are in European and American museums. American Museum of Natural History*
Size: About 14½'' by 15½''
Materials: Mono, No. 18 canvas; Persian wool, used in single threads.

Continental and Basketweave stitches are used for this design. In reading the
design chart, note that the background of the "cap" of the head A is medium moss
green; its symbol (/) has been omitted there to facilitate counting the dark moss
stitches. For the remainder of the head a blank square denotes pale green. The entire background of the work is turquoise (B); a three-stitch-wide border is of rose-
beige (C).

☒ Dark Moss Green   ◢ Medium Moss Green   • Light Green   ☐ Pale Green

A—Dark Moss Green   B—Turquoise   C—Rose-Beige

Each square of grid equals one stitch on canvas.

Drawing of a Benin bronze plaque.
Nigeria. Chicago Field Museum

BRONZE PATTERN

This is the "king's sarong with pattern" from part of a Benin bronze plaque found in the Field Museum, Chicago.

Size: About 17″ by 18½″

Materials: Mono, No. 10 mesh canvas; Persian wool, using full three-thread strand at a time.

Except for the center vertical panel, the background is worked in pale jade green. The background of the center panel—the checked one—is stitched in the next darker tone, light green on the chart. This background was not filled in so that the detail of the checks might be more easily counted.

Work in Basketweave and Continental stitches throughout.

Rose-Beige   Pale Green   Light Green   Pale Green   Pale Green   Rose-Beige

⊠ Dark Green   · Medium Green   ⊘ Light Green

Each square equals one stitch.

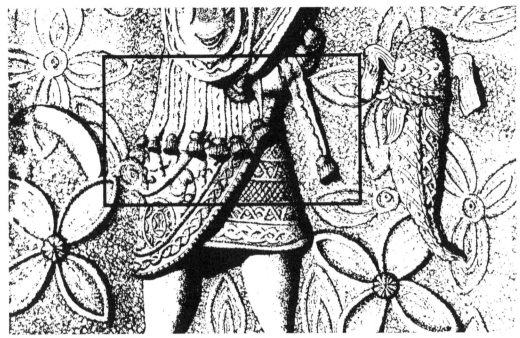

Drawing of a section of the Benin bronze plaque. Nigeria. Chicago Field Museum

BRONZE FRINGE

This is a detail of the Benin bronze plaque that I chose because I like the decorative tassels found on the king's sarong.

Size: About 12″ square

Materials: Mono, No. 12 mesh canvas; Persian wool, using two of its three threads at a time for the embroidery. Tassels are made with full strands.

Basketweave and Continental stitches are used for the entire work. Unshaded background squares of the chart are straw (A), bordered by rose-beige (B).

After the work has been blocked, make and attach tassels to the balls at each end of design motifs. Cut full strands of wool 5½″ to 6″ long. Fold at least eight of them in half over a ninth; square-knot it loosely to hold the bundle. Take a longer strand of wool and tie it about ½″ below the folded head of the bundle, leaving a very short end. Wrap the long end of the strand several times around the tassel, covering the tied end. With a tapestry needle, fasten the long end of wool at the top of the wrappings, then thread it through the center of the bundle and trim it and the tassel ends even. Undo the top knot. With a tapestry needle, thread one of its ends at a time to the wrong side of the canvas, directly under each ball—ends should be about four or five stitches apart. On the back of the canvas, cross the tie ends over each other. With sewing thread, fasten the crossing to backs of stitches as smoothly as possible, then trim neatly.

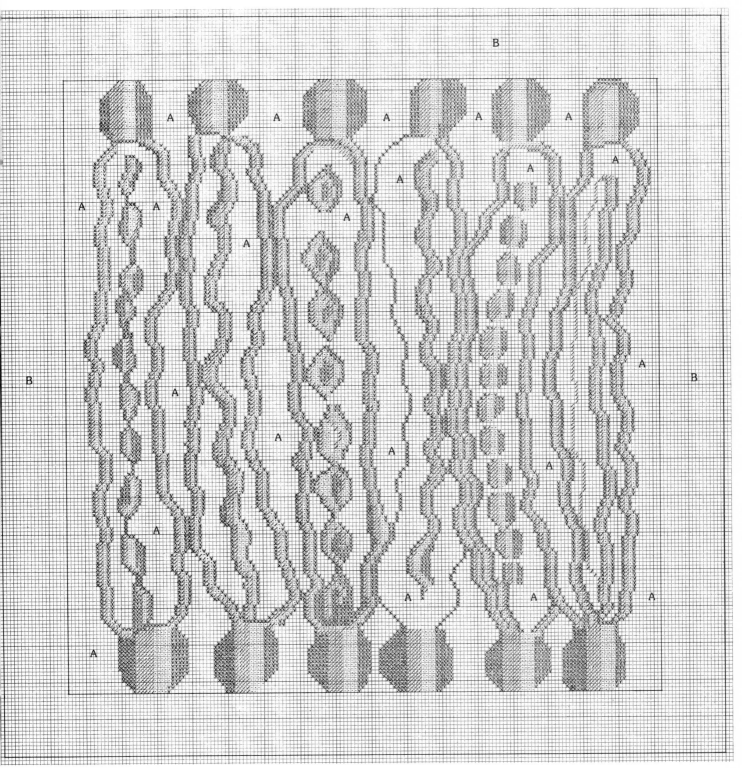

☒ Dark Moss ／ Medium Moss • Light Green ☑ Pale Green

A—Straw B—Rose-Beige

Drawing of background of a Benin bronze plaque. Nigeria. Chicago Field Museum

BRONZE FLOWERS

This clover-like flower was found in the background of a Benin bronze plaque. It is frequently used in other media as well. Field Museum, Nigeria
Size: About 18″ by 13″
Materials: Mono, No. 12 mesh canvas; Persian wool, using two of its three threads at a time.

The embroidery is Continental and Basketweave stiches throughout. For easier reading, the background check pattern on the design chart has been filled in only in part of the upper-left-hand corner; however, the entire background is to be worked in the same manner. The colors within each check are shaded from pale through medium green (from left to right) across the first horizontal row; they reverse in the next row to medium, light, and pale green. Alternate these rows for the height of the background.

Unshaded squares of the chart within flower petals and centers are stitched in straw (A). The twelve-stitch-wide border is done with rose-beige (B).

A—Straw   B—Rose-Beige

Pale Green

Light Green

Medium Green

Dark Green

Drawing of a section of a bronze plaque.
Field Museum at Benin, Nigeria

WHITE SLAVER

*This portrait of an early Portuguese slaver—the pipe and sword being represen-
tative of his trade—is a section of a bronze plaque seen at the Field Museum in
Benin, Nigeria.*
   Size: About 20½'' by 23½''
   Materials: Mono, No. 10 canvas; Persian wool, using full three-thread strands
throughout.

   The slaver himself is worked in Basketweave and Continental stitches. Note that
the unshaded areas of the figure are maize, including his pipe and swords. The entire
background is Interwoven stitch. The lengths of individual stitches within pattern
blocks around the slaver must be adjusted to his contours.
   For most hands this background stitch, worked with a full strand of Persian, will
completely cover a No. 10 canvas. Some very tense hands, however, may require
an additional thread. If so, separate the threads of the full strand before using. The
four threads will stitch more smoothly this way.

☐ Maize   ⬚ Ocher   ⊠ Chartreuse   Entire background is dark moss green.

Drawing of bronze fish plaque.
Benin, Nigeria. Chicago Field Museum

BRONZE FISH

This fish plaque from Benin, Nigeria, was cast in bronze and then hammered out to give a raised relief effect. Field Museum, Chicago

Size: About 14″ square.

Materials: Mono, No. 12 mesh canvas; Persian wool, used as described in instructions below.

The big fish is worked in three shades of cool (blue) gray—pale (the unshaded "C" areas in the diagram), medium, and dark, with accents of turquoise. Across the back fin, vertical stripes of dark gray Basketweave alternate with medium gray Brick stitch (two canvas threads high). The tail fins are done in the same way, except that the Brick stitch is horizontal; here, the turquoise is Basketweave. Use only two of the three threads of a Persian strand at a time.

Through the body of the big fish, scales are outlined with pale gray in an irregularly spaced and placed Cross stitch; it is worked over two canvas threads in each direction with two threads of wool at a time. Fill in the scales with medium gray horizontal Straight stitches in lengths to fit the shape of the scales, and with full three-thread strands of wool, and dark gray vertical Straight stitches in the same way. The

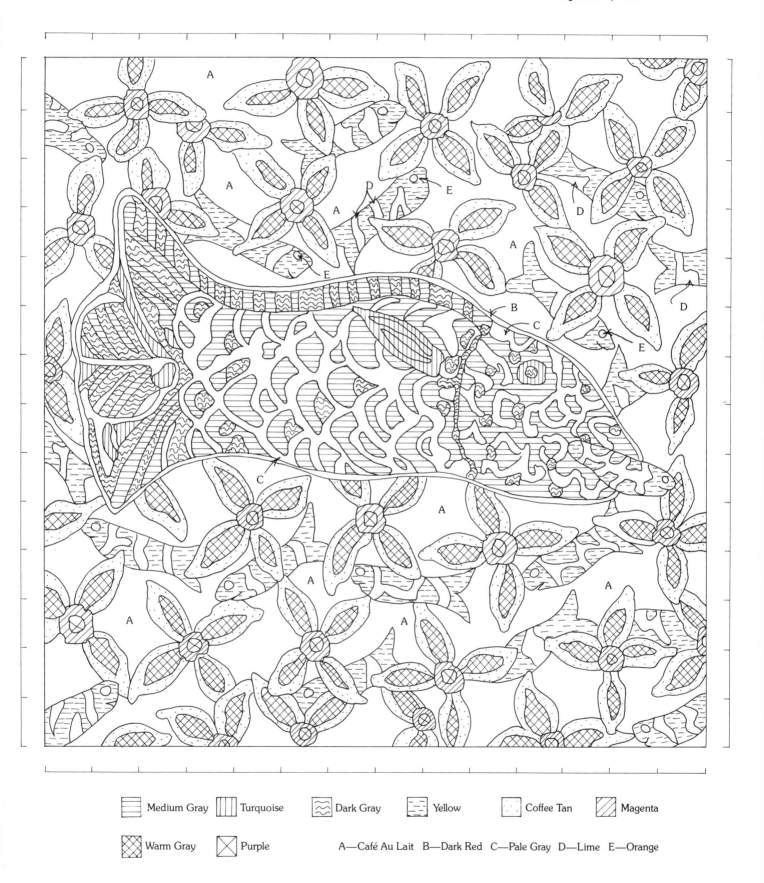

Medium Gray ⬛ Turquoise ⬛ Dark Gray ⬛ Yellow ⬛ Coffee Tan ⬛ Magenta

Warm Gray ⬛ Purple ⬛ A—Café Au Lait B—Dark Red C—Pale Gray D—Lime E—Orange

turquoise pectoral fin is done in Basketweave, and accented with short, horizontal Straight stitches—two threads of wool for each.

In the head, the dark and pale accents are done with Cross stitch as before, the medium gray areas are Basketweave. For the eye, turquoise Straight stitches radiate around vertical dark gray stitches of the eyeball—full strands of wool for each.

The big fish is outlined with two rows of dark red Continental stitch.

Small yellow fish are worked in Basketweave, with lime Mosaic stitch accents—two threads of wool at a time for each. For the eyes, orange French Knots are made with two threads of wool. Outline each little fish with dark gray back stitch—a single thread of wool, after the entire piece is worked.

A random choice of horizontal and vertical Straight stitches rims the flower petals—using a full strand of wool, the centers of which are warm, dark gray Basketweave. Centers of the flowers are 45° Straight Stitches—two threads of purple wool, ringed with horizontal and vertical Straight stitches done with a full strand of fuchsia.

The entire background is Upright Cross stitch, the horizontal cross topmost, worked with two threads of wool. Complete the piece with a row or two of Continental stitching in the background color.

BURLAP FISH—WALL HANGING

Size: About 28″ by 18″ finished

Materials: Burlap base fabric, natural; Persian wool, using full strand except as noted below, steel gray.

The big fish is Stem stitch except for French Knot dot detail in its head. Outline the eye rings, but French-knot the eyeball. Use only a single thread for Stem-stitching the little fish.

Work the flower petals in Chain stitch. Also Chain-stitch the outer ring of the flower centers, but Stem-stitch the inner ring and fill with French Knots.

BURLAP FISHSCALES

Size: Embroidered outer rectangle about 24″ by 13″ high; add at least 1½″ all around for fabric border

Materials: Burlap base fabric in natural; Persian wool, using full three-thread strand, steel gray.

No diagram is needed for the runner, since its design is an irregular repeat of the scale pattern across the back of the Burlap Fish (p. 58). Use that as a guide, drawing the scales freehand. The design can be worked to any desired proportion. Allow about 1¼″ between rectangular outline of the fishscales and the outer rectangle.

The entire design is worked in Stem stitch.

Sketch of rooster feathers

ROOSTER FEATHERS

I drew these three rooster-inspired drawings from a bronze rooster seen in Benin, Nigeria, because they lend themselves so well to the white on white bas-relief effect. Field Museum
   Size: Embroidered area about 22½″ by 14″

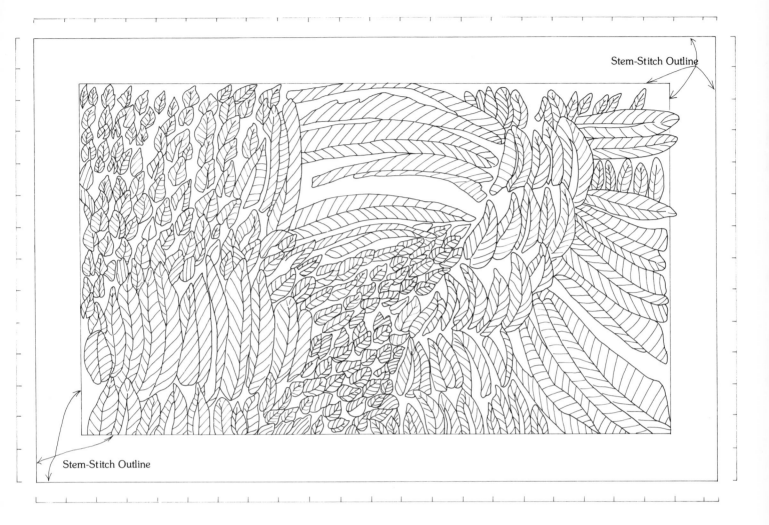

Stem-Stitch Outline

Stem-Stitch Outline

Sketch of rooster feathers frame

FEATHER FRAME

Size: Embroidered area about 15'' by 18''

Satin Stitch

Stem-Stitch   Satin Stitch

Drawing of rooster in bronze.
Benin, Nigeria. Chicago Field Museum

BRONZE ROOSTER

Size: Panel about 22½'' by 27''.

Materials: For each piece, medium-weight unbleached cotton fabric; eggshell Persian wool, using one of its three threads at a time.

In each of these embroideries, the feathers are done in very, very closely worked Satin stitch—even without understitching, there is a slight build-up of the embroidered texture. Heavy lines show the shapes of the feathers; fine lines indicate the directions of the stitches only. Some of the feathers have double center lines for their shafts; do not fill these spaces—allow the fabric to show through.

Feather Panel: The panel is bordered by two rows of Stem stitch, about 1¼'' apart all around.

Feather Frame: Embroider the irregular line around the feathers in Stem stitch.

Rooster: His body feathers are stitched in irregular tiers; only the larger plumes are worked individually. Using Diagonal Darning, fill the lobe under the rooster's beak and his leg shanks from claws to feathered area. When all other stitching has been done, Stem-stitch around the bird's back, the darned lobe, his breast, and legs down to the claws.

Stem-Stitch Outline

Diagonal Darning

Stem-Stitch
Outline

Stem-Stitch Outline

Stem-Stitch Outline

Diagonal Darning

Stem-Stitch Outline

Sketch of ivory leopard.
Benin, Nigeria. Chicago Field Museum

BENIN LEOPARD

Africa abounds in "airport" ivory carvings so one must draw on the museums to find favorites such as this leopard carving with its monolithic shape and delicate surface. Benin, Nigeria. Field Museum, Chicago
   Size: About 16″ by 14″
   Materials: Mono, No. 14 mesh canvas; Persian wool, using two of its three threads at a time.

Work in Basketweave and Continental stitches.

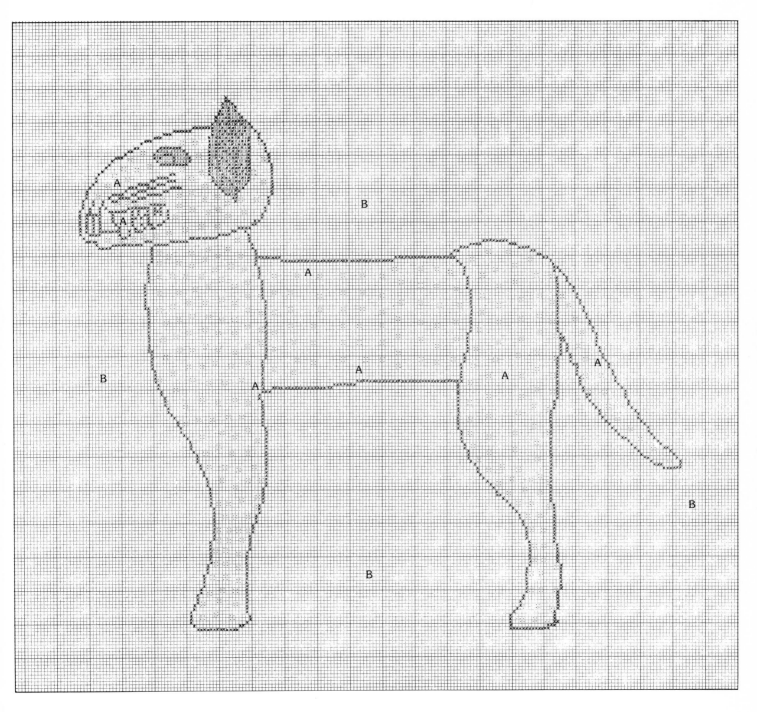

Each square of chart equals one stitch.

☒ Dark Rust ▯ White • Light Rust

A—Cream B—Slate

BENIN LEOPARD SPOT

Size: About 16″ square

Materials: Mono, No. 14 mesh canvas; Persian wool, using two of its three threads at a time. Many hands will require a full three-thread strand of the wool for covering the canvas adequately when working the Bargello border.

Stitches of the Bargello pattern are worked over three horizontal threads of the canvas; the four-color repeat is one-way throughout the border.

The spots are done in Basketweave; alternating Mosaic stitch is the background. Stitches that slant from the lower left toward the upper right are worked in white, those from lower right to upper left are done with cream. This "blending" of color produces a subtle ivory tone.

Upper-Right-Hand Quarter

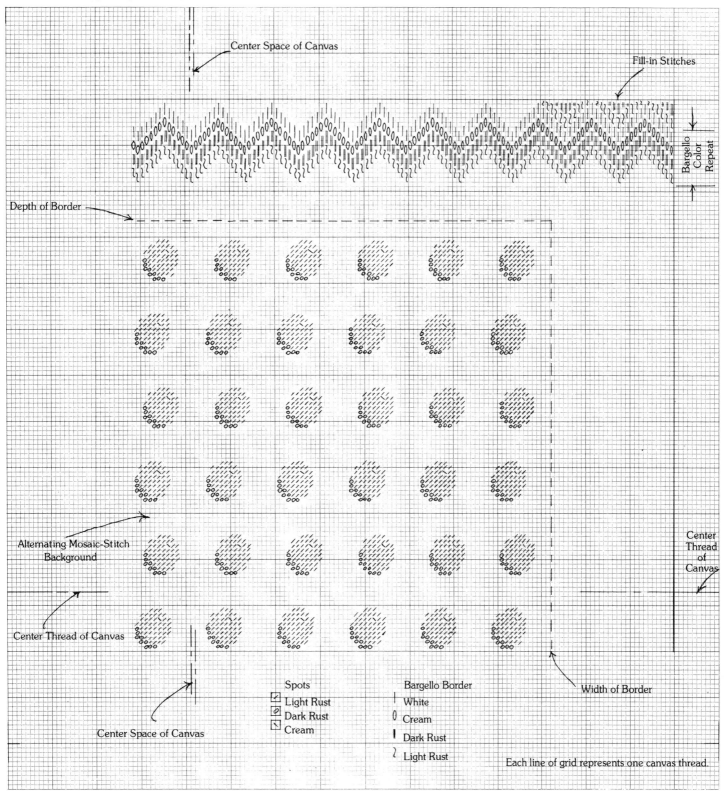

Center Space of Canvas

Fill-in Stitches

Bargello Color Repeat

Depth of Border

Alternating Mosaic-Stitch Background

Center Thread of Canvas

Center Space of Canvas

Center Thread of Canvas

Width of Border

Spots
☑ Light Rust
☑ Dark Rust
☑ Cream

Bargello Border
| White
0 Cream
❙ Dark Rust
⟩ Light Rust

Each line of grid represents one canvas thread.

Sketch of an ivory armband. Nigeria

NIGERIAN PUFF

The use of the over and under motifs in this ivory armband have fascinated carvers and this author. Nigeria

Size: Designed to cover the sides of a hassock, this work measures about 60″ across and about 18″ high. Here a continuous 18″ (190 stitches on our canvas) has been adapted from the sample embroidery.

Materials: Mono, No. 10 mesh canvas; Persian wool, using full three-thread strands.

Note: The top of the hassock has not been included in our design chart.

Use Basketweave and Continental stitches for this design. For a single repeat (to be used as a wall hanging, perhaps), work from line A-A′ on the design chart across to B-B′.

If, however, a hassock cover is planned, first have the upholsterer who will complete the hassock draw a pattern for it. The pattern should include allowance for possible drawing-in from the stitching, shrinkage in blocking, and seam allowance. If a solid-color needlepoint top will also be stitched, get a coordinating pattern for it at the same time.

Mark the center of the hassock pattern at the top edge. Transfer the pattern size to the canvas, again marking the center at the top edge with thread or a hard pencil. From that center point on the canvas, count 95 threads toward the right (½ repeat). From that last thread, continuing toward the right, count the number of full repeats needed for this half of the pattern. There will probably be space at the right-hand end of your pattern for a part-repeat. Count the number of threads in that space. On the design chart, count that number of squares to the right of line B-B′; draw a vertical line to the bottom edge of the chart along that row of squares, for the starting line of stitching.

From the starting line on the chart, begin your stitching at the right-hand end of the canvas pattern. Continue to chart line B-B′, then work continuous repeats from A-A′ to B-B′ across the canvas, ending with a part-repeat from A-A′ at the left-hand end of the canvas pattern.

Center of Repeat

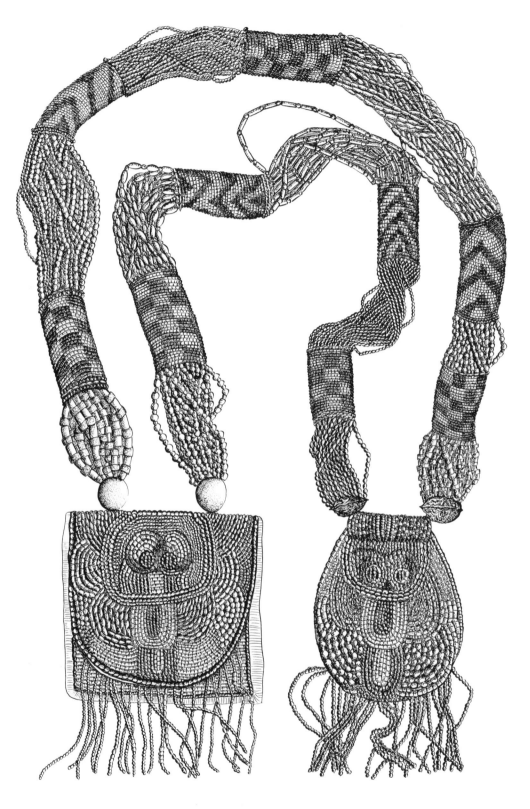

Sketch of a double money purse, beaded.
Nigeria. Author's collection

NIGERIAN DOUBLE PURSE

Seeing this Nigerian beaded money purse posed a question in my mind: Was it to be worn around the chief's neck or around the chief paymaster's neck? No one could tell me. Author's collection

Size: On our canvas the larger pouch is about 6'' square, the smaller about 4½'' by 5½''; each neck strap slide is about 3'' by 4''

Materials: Mono, No. 10 mesh canvas; Persian wool, using full three-thread strands for needlepoint, rug wool to harmonize with needlepoint colors for neck strapping; fabric for the backs of the bags, fabric to line each piece of needlepoint and the backs of the bags; sewing threads, fabric glue; optional: buttons for closures.

Embroider Squares I, II, III, and IV in Basketweave and in Continental stitch where necessary.

When pieces have been blocked, cut them from the canvas, leaving a ⅝'' canvas margin all around each square for seam allowance. Secure cut edges with glue, placing an extra dab at each corner of each piece just outside the needlework.

For patterns, trace the outlines of each needlework square; add ⅝'' seam allowance all around each one. Cut out the bag backs for Squares I and II, including seam allowance. Hold bag back and corresponding needlework right sides together. Keeping as close to the needlework as possible, back-stitch around the sides and bottom of each bag. Trim corners to within about ¼'' of stitching. Around the open top edge, turn seam allowance to wrong side; catch-stitch or hem it in place. At the side seams of each bag, with Persian wool make sturdy Buttonhole-stitch loop of about 1½'', at top edge, as for a belt—but keep ends close together near the seams. Turn bags right side out.

On wrong sides, seam front and back of each lining together, leaving tops open. Turn seam allowance around top edges to wrong side, baste in place. Insert linings into bags, hem top edges to tops of bags, matching side seams.

Prepare Strap Slides (Squares III and IV): Turn canvas margins of each piece to the wrong side along edges a-a', a'-b', and b-b', leaving a-b open and flat. Turn corresponding seam allowance of the linings to the wrong side in the same way, also leaving a side open. With wrong sides facing, hem linings to each side except along a-b; lining should cover the canvas margin. Baste it in place.

Neck Strap: Depending on the thickness of your particular rug wool, you will need about six, maybe more strands; each should be twice desired length of neck strap, plus about 3'' for knotting ends.

Place bags face up on a table, the desired length of neck strap apart, openings toward each other. One at a time, lace half of the strap strands through corresponding loops of each bag, and tie ends in a square knot. Repeat with other half of wool lengths through loops on opposite sides of the bags. Now stagger the knots of each strand, so that half of them will be spread between about 4″ and 7″ from Bag I. Arrange the remaining knots in the same fashion, the same distances from Bag II.

Take one of the slides, wrap it around a knotted area of the strands, overlapping hemmed edge a′-b′ on unfinished a-b canvas margin. Neatly hem in place so that needlepoint at least meets needlepoint, or slightly covers it. Repeat for other knotted section of the strap.

If desired, make thread loops at top center of each lining edge; sew buttons to bag fronts to correspond, for closure.

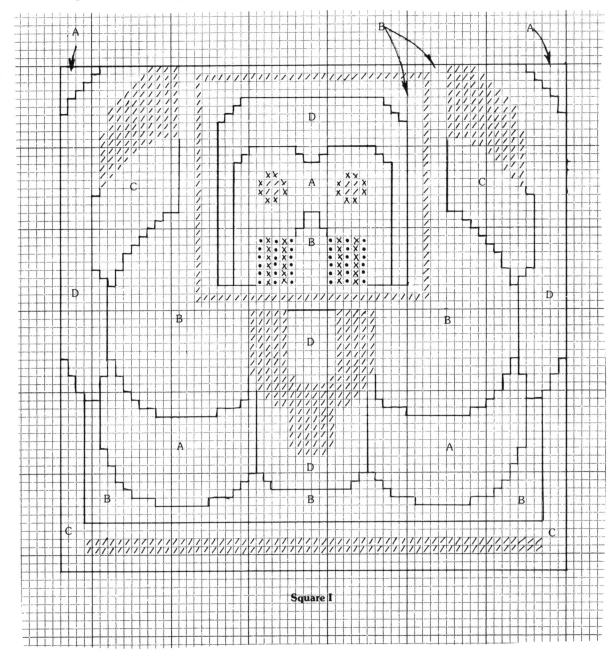

Square I

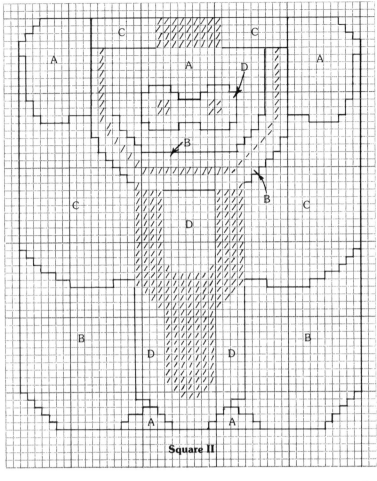

Square II

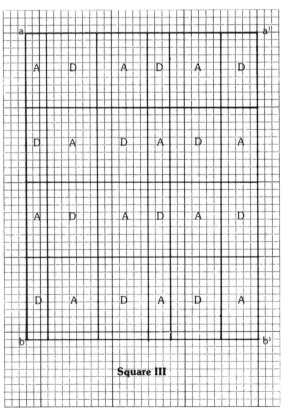

Square III

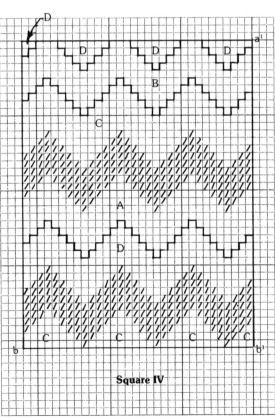

Square IV

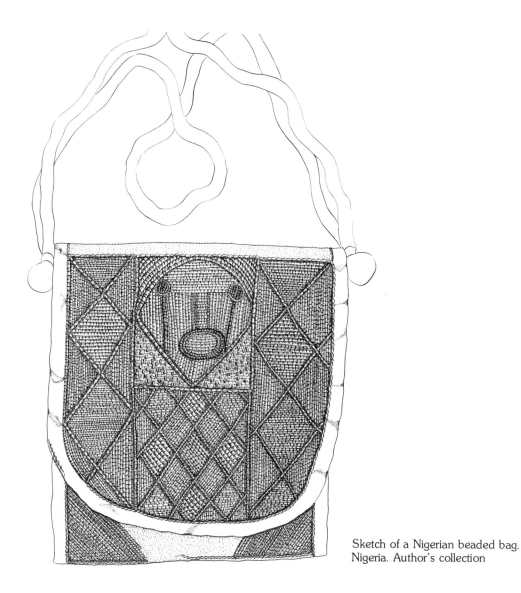

Sketch of a Nigerian beaded bag.
Nigeria. Author's collection

NIGERIAN BEADED BAG

I like to draw beaded things and this Nigerian beaded bag with its mysterious pattern was irresistible. Author's collection

Size: About 12″ wide by 12″ high

Materials: Mono, No. 10 mesh canvas; Persian wool using full three-thread strands.

Work the design in Basketweave, using Continental for lines that are only one stitch wide or high.

Colors

A—Chartreuse	D—Mustard	G—Light Maize
B—Kumquat	E—Dark Steel Blue	H—Medium Blue
C—Pale Blue	F—Gray	I—Rose-Beige

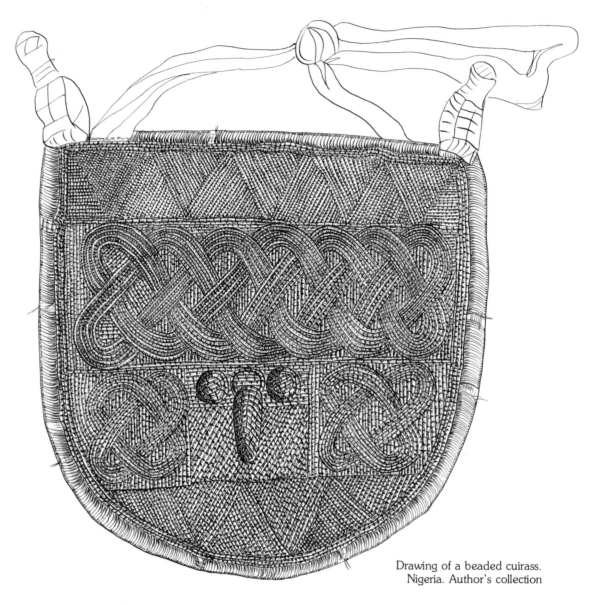

Drawing of a beaded cuirass.
Nigeria. Author's collection

NIGERIAN BEADED CUIRASS

Beads convert to needlepoint so completely that I chose this Nigerian beaded cuirass as one of my favorites.
Size: About 11″ by 11¼″
Materials: Mono, No. 10 mesh canvas; Persian wool, using full three-thread strands.

The major portion of this design can best be worked in Basketweave; Continental stitch will be needed for parts of the braid pattern.

Colors
A—Blue B—Maize C—Taupe D—Sand
E—Rose-Beige F—Puce G—Eggshell H—Dark Mustard

Puce • Eggshell Dark Mustard

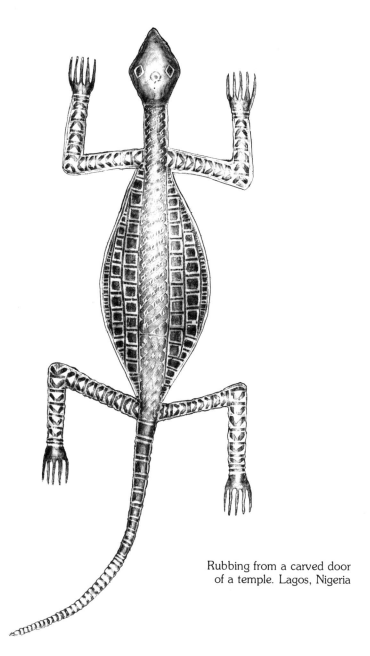

Rubbing from a carved door
of a temple. Lagos, Nigeria

LAGOS RUG

This rubbing from a carved door of a temple in Lagos, Nigeria, was made by the ambassador's wife for my son Dek. It makes a beautiful rug. Author's collection
Size: About 24″ by 36″
Materials: No. 5 double-mesh canvas; Paternayan rug wool.

The rug is worked in Continental and Basketweave stitches. The lower half is the reverse of the top, except for the horizontal bars which cross the diagonal-patterned strips. Those are placed at random along the length of each of the strips.

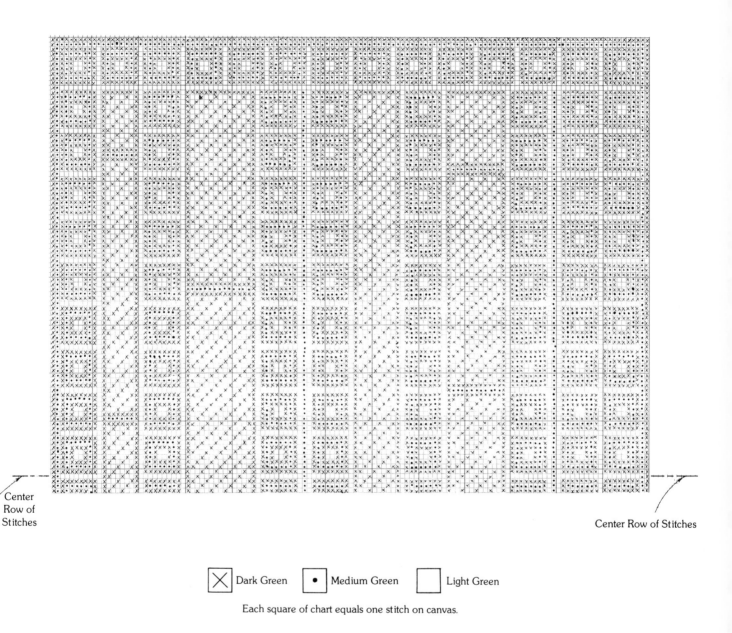

Center
Row of
Stitches

Center Row of Stitches

⊠ Dark Green   • Medium Green   ☐ Light Green

Each square of chart equals one stitch on canvas.

One-Half of Rug

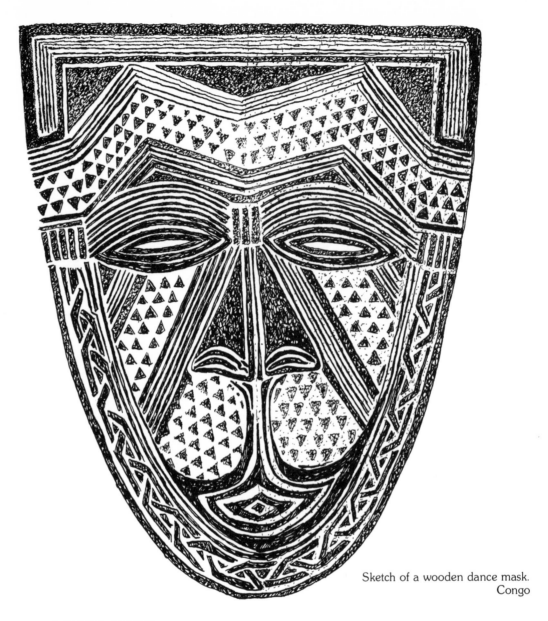

Sketch of a wooden dance mask.
Congo

CONGO MASK

A book on Africa must have a mask, and this wooden dance mask from the Congo is ritualistic in purpose.

Size: About 14½'' by 17¼''

Materials: Mono, No. 14 canvas; Persian wool, using two of three threads at a time.

Basketweave and Continental stitches are used. The black and white borders are each six stitches wide.

□ White   Each square of grid represents one stitch.
· Black

Sketch of Bushmen mural on rock face. Sethslabatebe, Lesotho

BUSHMAN HUNT

In Sethslabatebe, Lesotho, I walked out on the high ledge to see the painting of these Bushmen on the rock face but nearly lost my nerve inching back.

Size: About 14½'' by 14''

Materials: Putty tan cotton fabric, medium weight; Persian wool, using one of its three threads at a time.

Almost a Split-stitch workout—unless otherwise specified, it is used for both filling and outlines. Fine lines within each human, animal, and fantasy form show the directions of stitching only. This is usually parallel to the height of the figure, following its contours, and in colors indicated on the diagram.

Note, however, that the upper-left-hand hippo is stitched horizontally from hind quarters to head with white (B). The legs are Satin-stitched. Outline the entire animal in brown (A) Stem stitch.

Other working pointers: After shading the large rhino (below the hippo) from canteloupe (C) through bittersweet (D) to rust (E), outline the top of him (from snout, across his back, and around his hindmost leg—or dotted line to dotted line) with B; complete the rhino with A Outline stitch around his bottom parts.

The center-field, right-hand beast has a narrow band of B Satin stitch across his top, then D Satin stitch all around it and his B body. A Outline stitch completes the animal.

Colors

A—Dark Brown B—White C—Canteloupe D—Bittersweet E—Rust

Unless otherwise specified, the embroidery is all split stitch.

The bull at lower right has A Satin stitch only, around his B body and head, which has large D spots. His tail is a line of A Outline stitch over a line of Stem stitch; the bushy part of his tail is Straight stitch, all A.

A and B mounds between beasts and near the lower edge are just that. Though done in Satin stitch, they are padded with understitching (small Running stitches) to raise their surface.

The B terrain line is composed of alternate rows of outline and Stem stitches, for a braided effect.

Outline the entire scene with A Outline stitch.

Sketch of Rondavel hut, outer wall decoration in field stone. Lesotho

LESOTHO LEAF

In Lesotho this Rondavel hut, decorated with fieldstone, made very comfortable sleeping for my son Seth, but luckily nobody invited me in because the smoke from the fire hangs directly at eye level.

Size: About 14¼″ by 15″

Materials: Mono, No. 10 mesh canvas; Persian wool, using full three-thread strand at a time.

A—Steel Gray   B—Dark Gold

The entire design is stitched in Interwoven Straight stitches. Therefore the lengths of stitches within a pattern-stitch block must be adjusted to the contours of the leaves and stems during the course of the work.

For better finish, outline the entire piece with one or two rows of Continental stitch when the design has been completed.

Sketch of chief's fan
red flannel appliquéd on cowhide.
Benin, Nigeria. Chicago Field Museum

CHIEF'S FAN

This chief's fan, made from cowhide and appliquéd with red flannel (a favorite trade good), was used more for insect shooing than for cooling. Field Museum, Chicago

Size: 12″ by 11¾″

Materials: Red, medium-weight cotton fabric; Persian wool, using two of its three threads at a time.

The left-hand half of the diagram for this work approximates its finished appearance; the right-hand side shows the design's basic structure. Except for centering lines at top and bottom, all fine lines on the diagram indicate the directions of stitching only. All areas without fine lines or circles are background fabric showing through the tracery.

First with steel gray (A), embroider the tracery skeleton with Split stitch, which for the most part follows the contours of its structure. With dark brown (B) outline the tracery (all heavy lines on the diagram) in Stem stitch. Small circles represent bright gold (E) French Knots, worked right over the A stitches on both sides of the skeleton.

Around the tracery, fill in the Stem-stitch background with alternate lines of eggshell (C) and pale gray (D), so closely worked that the base fabric is completely covered. Finally, outline the fan with B Stem stitch.

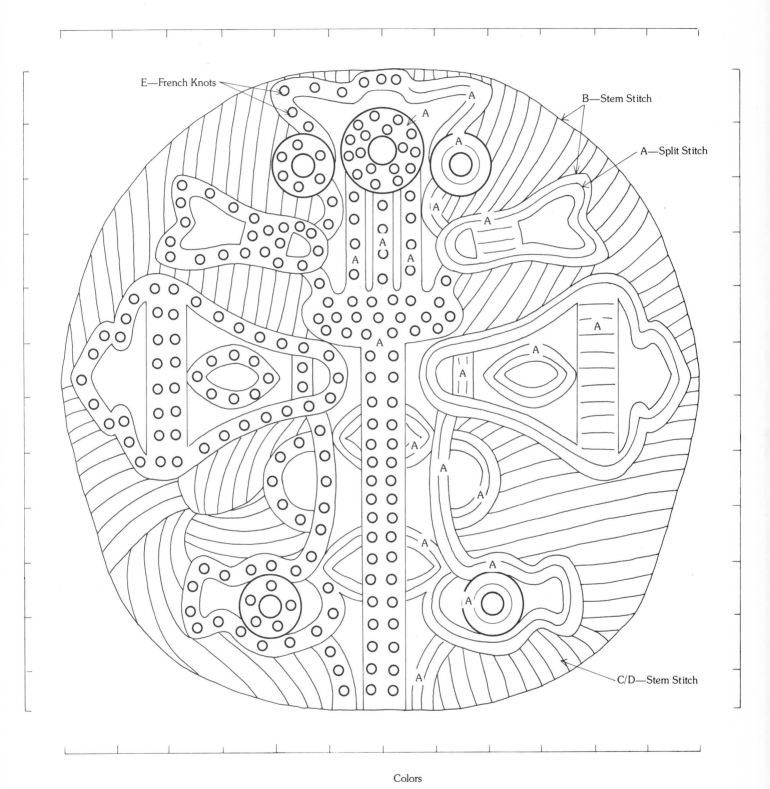

E—French Knots

B—Stem Stitch

A—Split Stitch

C/D—Stem Stitch

Colors

A—Steel Gray   B—Darkest Brown   C—Eggshell   D—Pale Blue-Gray   E—Bright Gold

Sketch of zebra. Nairobi, Kenya

PAPILIO ZEBRANCUS

This is based on a sketch of zebra as I saw them on the plains of Kenya moving in a vast kaleidoscope pattern that occasionally separated into individual animals.
Size: Embroidery about 17½″ by 12½″
Materials: Gray, medium-weight cotton or linen fabric; Persian wool, using one of its three threads at a time.

In the diagram for this design, jagged-edged black and eggshell stripes represent "encroaching" embroidery stitches. For the most part these are Satin stitch. But Split stitch is used in the same way, where a stripe is too wide for a single row of stitches. Fine lines within clouds and creature indicate the directions of stitching only.

After stripings have been completed, first outline the wings with black Split stitch (heavier outline on the diagram), then Stem-stitch a line of black (dotted line) above the tops of the wings. "Body" and clouds are not outlined.

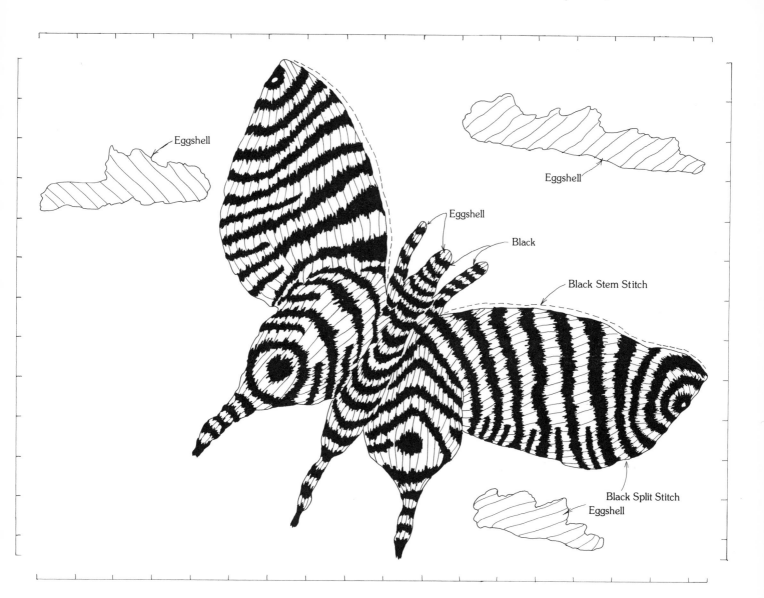

Eggshell

Eggshell

Eggshell

Black

Black Stem Stitch

Black Split Stitch

Eggshell

Sketch of giraffe.
Kenya, Nairobi

ORNITHOPTERA GIRAFFICUS

On the plains of Kenya, giraffes would spread their legs (which topped my head) and in two or three jerks would fall to a split position in order to eat the grass below.

Size: Embroidery about 13½″ by 15½″

Materials: Gray, medium-weight cotton or linen fabric; Persian wool, using one of its three threads at a time.

Within the diagram, fine lines indicate the various directions of stitching only; heavy dotted lines represent Chain-stitch outline; and saw-toothed lines show "encroaching" stitches between colors. Because of the lengths of stitches, keep tension easy.

The giraffe-like body is done in Satin stitch. The upper part is copper (A) around dark rust (C) spots; the face is outlined with A Stem stitch. Ears are spice (D). The lower body is striated—colors are indicated on the diagram.

Background of each wing is tawny peach (B) Satin stitch. Upper parts of each spot are A, lower sections are encroaching C—all in Satin stitch. Between the upper wings is a narrow band of D Split stitch. D Chain stitch outlines all but the head of the mammal fly.

The tree is all D—Satin stitch for foliage, Split stitch for the trunk.

Colors

A—Copper   B—Tawny Peach   C—Dark Rust   D—Spice

Sketch of cheetah
Nairobi, Kenya

POLYGONIA LEOPARDUS

This cheetah could outrun my jeep on the bumpy plains of Kenya.
Size: Embroidery about 15½'' by 11½''
Materials: Gray, medium-weight cotton or linen fabric; Persian wool, using one of its three threads at a time.

Fine lines within the diagram show the directions of filling stitching only; outlines define shapes of areas only; all heavy dotted lines indicate Stem stitching.

Leopard-like spots are done in closely worked Satin stitch, first with gold (A). With spice (C), shade a central portion of each spot with a few Straight stitches. They are worked directly over the A's and in the same directions.

Filling around the spots is light gold (B) Straight stitching, irregular and encroaching, sparsely covering the fabric. Lower wing sections are stitched in chevron fashion as shown.

In the "body" portion of the mammal-fly, horizontal bands are C Satin stitch, as is the inverted "U" around its head. Ears are filled with C Stem stitch, and both ears and eyes are Stem stitch, outlined with C Satin stitch, as are the various sections of wings and body.

Blades of wild grass at the bottom of the piece are green (D) Stem stitch.

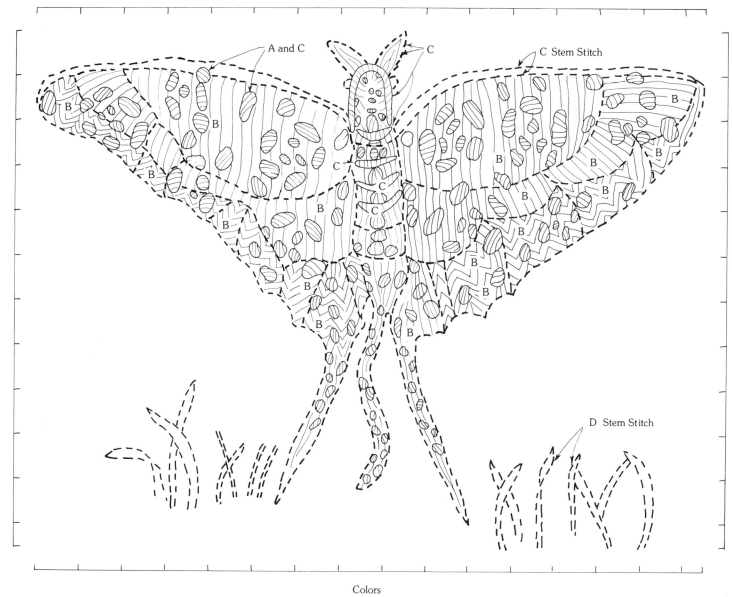

A and C

C

C Stem Stitch

B

B

B

B

B

B

B

B

B

C

C

C

B

B

B

B

B

B

B

B

D Stem Stitch

Colors
A—Gold B—Light Gold C—Spice D—Grass

CHEETAH SKIN

Size: About 14″ square

Materials: Mono, No. 10 mesh canvas; Persian wool, used in three-thread strands at a time, blended as described below.

The skin is worked entirely in Brick stitch, each full stitch covering four canvas threads. The lengths of stitches must of course be adjusted to the contours of the cheetah spots.

The darkest parts of the spots are connected with blended strands of wool, indicated on the design diagram by shading, and designated by three letters. Each letter denotes one thread of a color as listed in the chart below, which are to be used at one time. The spots themselves are worked with full strands of midnight brown (H) only.

Background colors are shaded from light to dark in twelve vertical stripes about ⅞″ wide (nine stitches across on our canvas), and a thirteenth band—the darkest— which fills the remaining 3½″ across the canvas.

In twelve of the stripes, the colors are blends of two or three different tones, as in the spot "filling." And, as above, each of the colors has a letter designation. Three letters denote the colors that make up the blended strands to be used within the stripes (separated by dotted lines on the diagram). The lightest stripe is worked with a full strand of oatmeal (A) only.

See the color designation list below and the chart of blends for each of twelve stripes.

COLOR DESIGNATIONS

A—Oatmeal
B—Light Café au Lait
C—Light Golden Tan
D—Camel
E—Toffee
F—Tobacco

G—Bitter Chocolate
H—Midnight Brown
W—Copper
X—Apricot
Y— Soft Peach
Z— Pale Peach

BLENDS FOR STRIPES

Stripe 1: EEW
Stripe 2: DEW
Stripe 3: DEX
Stripe 4: DDX
Stripe 5: CDX
Stripe 6: CDY

Stripe 7: CCY
Stripe 8: BCY
Stripe 9: BCZ
Stripe 10: BBZ
Stripe 11: ABZ
Stripe 12: AAB
Stripe 13: AAA

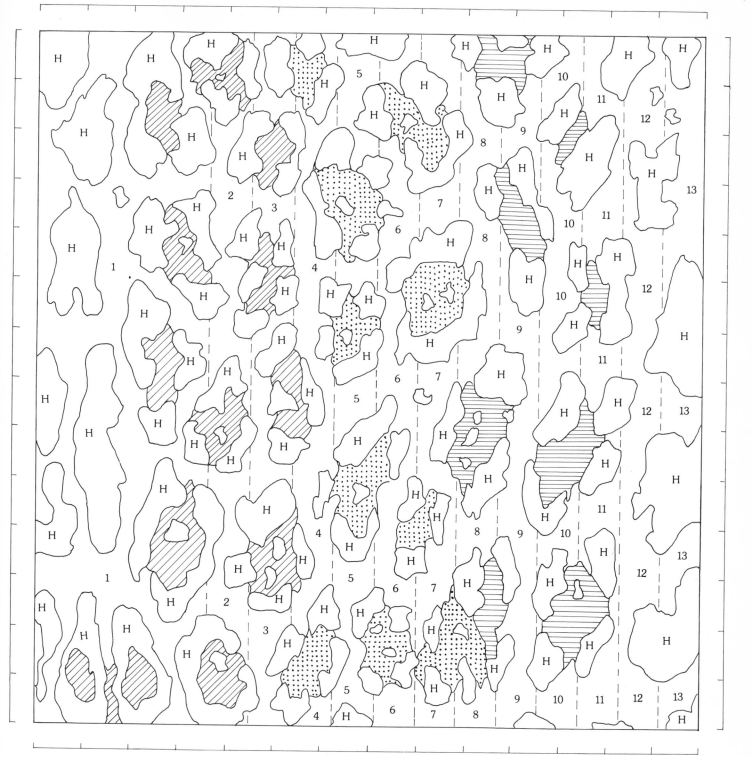

Spot Color Mixes
Each letter denotes one thread of colors used together as strands.

⋯⋯ FEX   ▨ FGW   ☰ FEY

See instructions for color key and colors within background stripes 1–13.

Based on Akan chief's sarong of appliqué work. Private collection

AKAN QUILT

The inspiration for this crib quilt is a man's sarong.
Size: About 35½'' by 52½''
Materials / Cloth: Colorfast, pre-shrunk cotton or cotton-blend fabrics, both prints and solids of your choice. All the cloth should be of about the same weight and opaque. Although this quilt was done in blues and white for the top and henna (or brick red) for the lining, there is no need to limit your choice of colors or the number of them.

Appliqué Motifs: Odd sizes of assorted cottons will be needed.
Blocks: Twenty-four assorted pieces, 9½'' square.
Lining: The backing fabric should be a minimum of 38'' by 55''.
If the quilt will be used only as a bedspread, the fabrics can be somewhat textured; but for a coverlet, smooth fabrics will be more comfortable and pleasant.

Embroidery Thread: This quilt was embroidered and stitched with DMC Retors à Broder No. 4; brick was used for the embroidery of squares and corner tufting, blue and white for the tufts within each block to contrast with each background. However, depending on the weight of the fabrics for your quilt, Perle Cotton No. 3 or No. 5, or even six-strand floss can be used—full or part strand as needed.

Padding: Cotton or polyester batting, 35½'' by 52½''—the finished size of the quilt.

Miscellaneous: Sewing thread to match the lining, and plenty of basting thread. And of course the materials for enlarging and transferring the block designs (see pp. 6 and 7).

Each finished block is 8½'' square. Use all of the motifs shown, repeating favorites to make up the twenty-four blocks, or choose one or a few for your entire quilt. Plan the use of your fabrics, contrasting solids with prints, solids with solids, or even pattern with pattern as desired.

Enlarge each square diagram to 8½''. Draw another line about ¼'' outside each appliqué motif to be used, for seam allowance. On the reverse side of the drawing, go around both motif outlines with transfer pencil. Note: If motifs will be appliquéd to the blocks with closely worked Buttonhole stitch, no seam allowance is necessary.

Press all fabrics before using.

Transfer the motif outlines to the wrong side of the appliqué fabrics; this will prevent the pencil color from showing on the right side, and when a print is used the outlines will be more easily followed. Turn the seam allowance of the motifs to the wrong side, notching, slashing, and mitering as needed for a smooth and flat edge; baste in place.

Cut out the 9½'' squares for each block. Center motifs on the squares as in the drawings; baste in place. With embroidery thread, Satin-stitch around the motif (or Buttonhole-stitch if desired). Since motifs have a finished edge, Satin stitches need be only close enough to keep the seam allowance in place; our quilt was stitched closely enough to form a solid-color outline of the motif.

Plan the layout of the blocks. Assemble them first in horizontal rows of four across each, using the full ½'' allowance. If desired, they can be pre-stitched together by machine on the wrong side. Or turn the seam allowance to the wrong side and baste it down. In either case, on the right side Satin-stitch or overcast the blocks together with embroidery thread along their side edges. On the wrong side, press the seams open and flat. Trim the top and bottom corners of the seam allowances between blocks, but not at the outside edges. Join the rows of blocks in the same way, being sure to match seams. Press the seams open as before. Do not trim the seam allowance around the outside edges of the quilt top.

Spread the lining wrong side up on a flat surface. On it mark the finished size (35½'' by 52½'') of the quilt with basting stitches so that there is a margin of cloth 1¼'' wide all around the basting. This margin will form the binding of the quilt later on. Spread the batting on the lining, centering it; smooth and pat it in place—do not pull it taut and thin.

Starting from the center each time, baste out to each of the four edges and diagonally to each of the four corners, to fix the batting to the lining. In the same way, do a few more rows of basting—horizontal and vertical—on either side of the centers. This will help to keep the batting from moving around during the remainder of the finishing. If necessary, trim the batting to the size of the basted outline on the lining.

Now spread the quilt top, right side up, on the batting, being sure to center it. (The quilt top IS smaller than the batting—do not be alarmed.) In the same way as for the batting, baste the quilt top through the batting to the lining. Then, starting from the center each time, baste along each line of blocks in all four directions, and finally around the edges. Do not remove bastings until the quilt has been completed.

Tufting: Again, work from the center out in each direction. Thread a large-eyed, sharp needle with two strands of appliqué embroidery thread. Start in a corner of a block. Leaving an end of about 2'' on the top, take the needle straight down through the three layers and out on the right side of the lining. Be careful not to shift the positions of the layers. Bring the needle up and out in the diagonally opposite corner of a neighboring block, taking a short stitch on the lining's right side. Repeat the stitch process next to the first one. Pull both ends of the threads to tighten the stitches. Tie the ends in a square knot and trim to desired length. Repeat the tuft at each four-corner joining of the blocks and at the midpoint of each block seam. Do not tuft the ends of the seam at the outside edges yet. Using the same or desired colors, tuft each block in at least six or eight or more spots around the appliqués. Frequent tufting will keep the batting from slipping, ensuring more comfort and warmth and greater wear. (We used as little tufting as possible for our quilt, for photographic reasons.)

If it is not already so, now trim the lining margin to 1¼'' around the basted mark. Trim the corners to within ½'' from the basted corner. Fold the ½'' allowance

toward the quilt over the batting; pin in place. Then bring adjacent sides of the margin together to form a miter at the corners—the sides are folded over the quilt top on the basted marking. Neatly overcast or blind-stitch the miters together—be sure they are firmly stitched—to within ½'' of the margin edge. Turn under ½'' allowance all around the margin edge, bringing it over the exposed batting onto the quilt top, overlapping its edge by ½''. Pin, then baste the binding to the top, making sure it is smooth. Hem in place all around, taking a few short stitches to reinforce the miter closing at the top. Now tuft the block seams just inside the binding. Remove all basting.

AKAN HAND PANEL

AKAN HEART PILLOW

Size: The embroidered outline is about 12½'' square; add at least 1½'' of base fabric around the square as border

Materials: White, medium-weight cotton fabric; Persian wool, using single thread throughout, black; for padding, polyester or cotton batting and thin white cotton backing fabric.

These pieces are done in Split-stitch filling, and outlined in Stem stitch. For a raised embroidery surface, stitch the filling first. Follow the contours of the hand and the hearts for three or four rows around, then complete the filling in the most convenient direction.

Next, baste the backing cloth around the wrong side of the embroidery so that it is smooth and somewhat taut, and extends beyond the motifs by about ⅝''. Then, working through both thicknesses of fabric, on the right side of the work outline the figures with Stem stitch, stuffing as you go:

For the hearts, start at a tip and work around, leaving about ¾'' open; do not end off the thread. With a pencil or knitting needle, force bits of stuffing between backing and the embroidery until motif is desired height. Pull backing taut again, pin in place, then complete the Stem-stitch outline.

Do the hand in a similar way. Start at the wrist and outline the thumb. Through spaces between basting stitches, force bits of batting in it. Continue around, stuffing each finger in turn after it is outlined. Leave an opening about 1'' wide at the top of the wrist, stuff the palm, then complete the closing stitching. Trim the backing to within about ¼'' of the embroidery.

Outline the square in Stem stitch.

AKAN FISH PILLOW

Size: About 10″ square
Materials: Mono, No. 10 mesh canvas; Persian wool, using full three-thread strand at a time.

The entire design is stitched in Basketweave and Continental stitches.

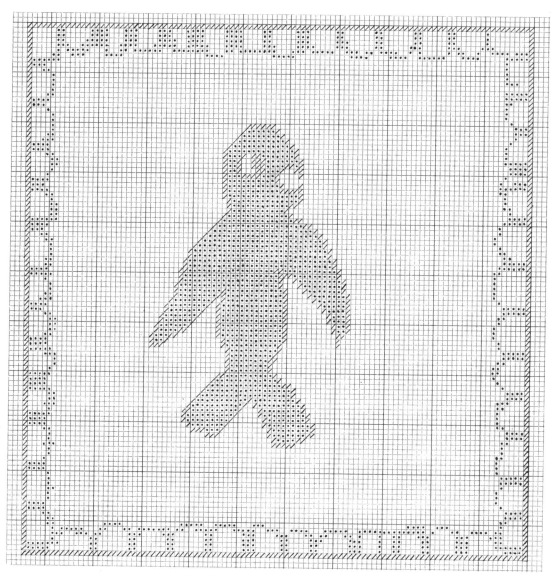

⧄ Dark Gray ⊡ Cranberry ☐ Pale Blue

Each square equals one stitch.

AKAN WHEEL PILLOW

Size: About 10″ square
Materials: Mono, No. 10 mesh canvas; Persian wool, full three-thread strands.

Work in Basketweave or Continental stitches as applicable.

A—Slate   B—Ice Blue   C (●)— Cranberry

AKAN LIZARD PILLOW

Size: About 7'' by 14½'
Materials: Mono, No. 10 mesh canvas; Persian wool, full three-thread strands.

Use Basketweave stitch for the entire piece.

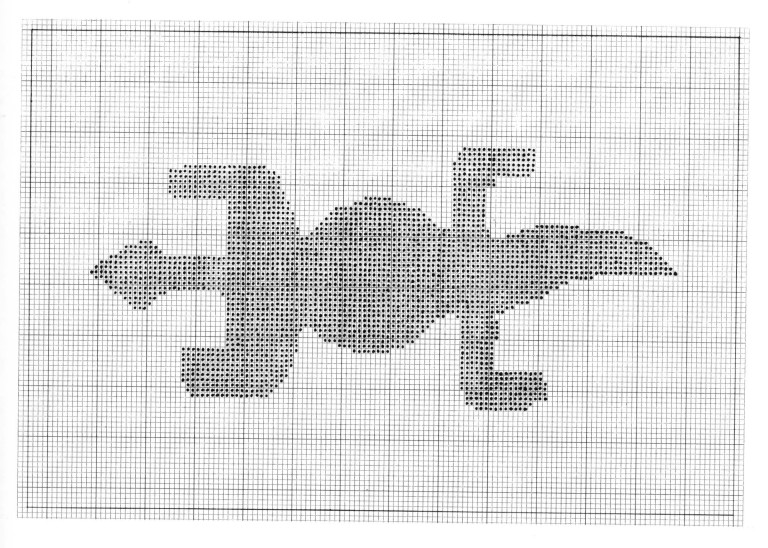

• White   □ Black

AKAN ELEPHANT PILLOW

Size: About 12½'' by 11''
Materials: Mono, No. 10 canvas; Persian wool, using full three-thread strands.

This entire small work can best be done in Basketweave.

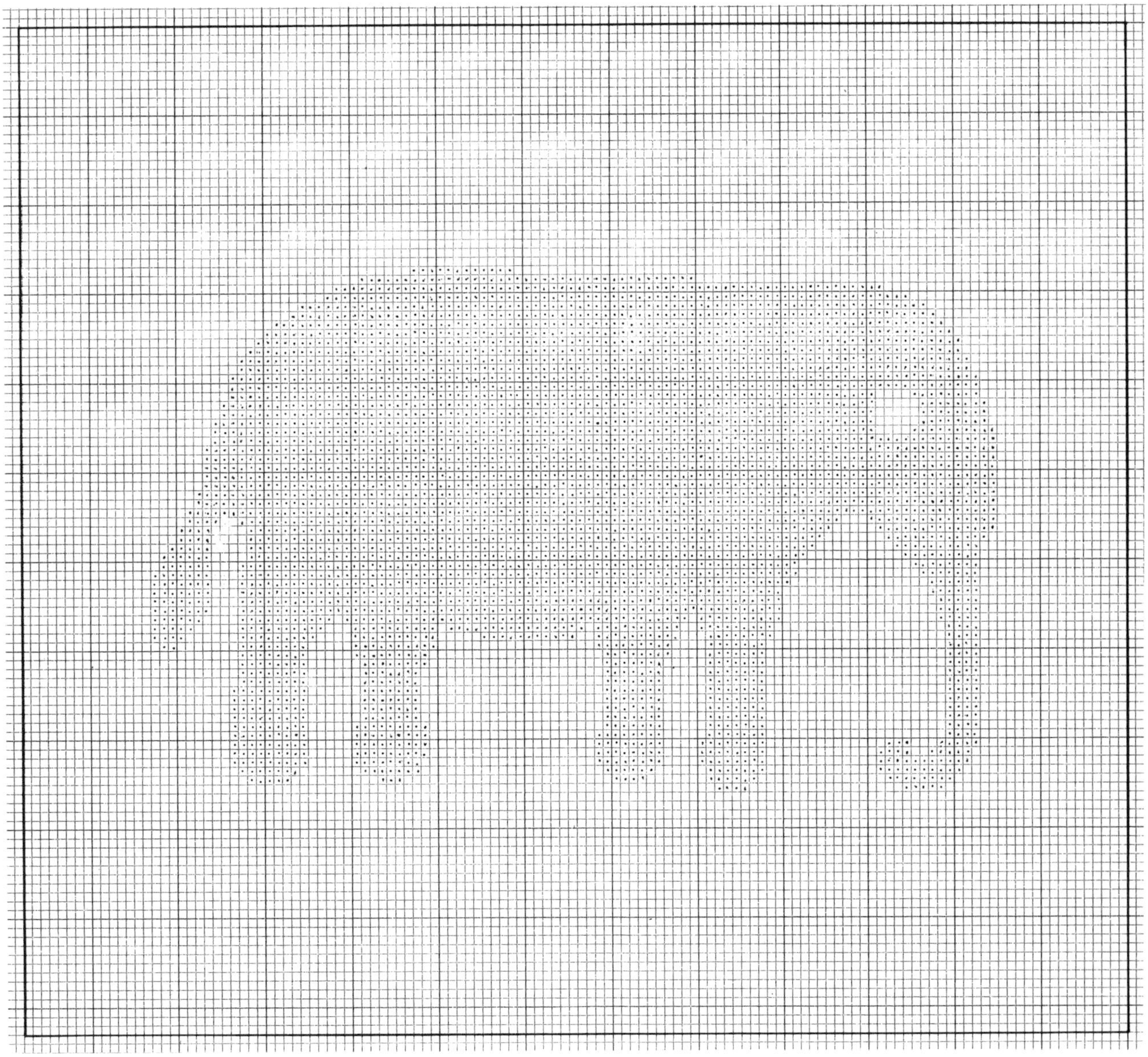

· Black   White

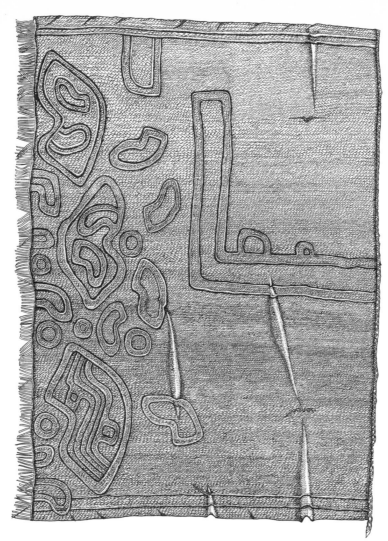

Sketch of a panel of raffia
from Kuba, Zaire

KUBA RAFFIA PANEL

This panel of raffia from Kuba, Zaire, was most likely a man's garment but the shadow patterns seem so right for a wall hanging.

Size: Finished, about 44″ by 62″

Materials: Natural burlap fabric a minimum of 43″ by 61″, heavy blue cotton for lining at least 48″ by 66″; natural heavy jute twine, scarlet Perle Cotton No. 3, carpet thread to match twine, basting cotton; large steel rug needle, about No. 20 tapestry needle for carpet thread, colorless fabric glue; rings for hanging the tapestry.

In the diagram for the hanging, the long dash line represents the finished cut edge of the burlap, and the dotted lines are stitching lines for the flat braid, which is about ⅝″ wide. The facing border of the hanging is in one with the lining.

Secure the cut edges of the burlap by machine or hand overcasting, or fabric glue before transferring design to it.

BRAID

For this hanging, five strands of twine were used to make each strip of braid. The simplest way to make this braid is to take five strands of heavy knitting yarn, each a different color and each about 12″ long. Staple an end of each strand to a small piece of cardboard; from the left, label them A, B, C, D, and E, as in the braid diagram. Since all braiding requires some tension, place a weight on the cardboard; or punch a hole in it, thread a piece of string through the hole, then attach it to a doorknob, a drawer knob, or the back of a chair.

The loose ends of A, B, and C go in your left hand; place D and E in your right hand. Hold the ends at just enough tension to keep the strands almost straight—there is no need to pull the yarns taut. Without dropping any strands, use thumb and forefinger to transfer one at a time from one hand to the other. Follow the diagram.

Step 1: With your right hand pass A over and across B and C, holding it in center position just to the left of D. Strands will now be B and C in your left hand, A, D, and E in your right hand.

Step 2: With your left hand take E across D and A, holding it to the right of B and C at center. Strands will now read from the left: B, C, E/A, D.

Step 3: B is now transferred from your left hand across C and E to center—strands are now C, E/B, A, D.

Step 4: D is moved across A and B to be held at center in your left hand—C, E, D/B, A.

Step 5: Take C across E and D to center it. Note that yarns are now, E, D, C/B, A—the reverse of their starting order.

Continue the same way with Steps 6–10, then repeat Steps 1–10 for desired length of each section of braid.

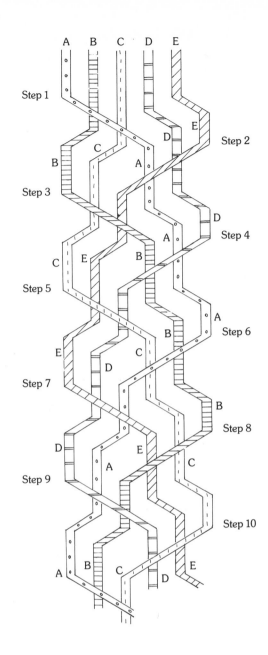

Finished Braid

ADVICE

Patching braid does not work well. It is better to work about 1½" to 3" more than estimated for each separate part of the design; trim the braid as needed when sewing each strip to the burlap.

Once the technique has been learned, there is no need for cardboard as a base. Simply wrap the strands together about 1" or so below their ends with carpet thread or string; tie string in a loop to hang on a knob. Work to within 1–2" of the other end and tie again.

In bulky knitting yarn, about 24" of each strand produced a little more than 17" of braid, with ample ends remaining. But the thicker the cords, the greater the lengths of it that will be needed per yard of braid; if thin yarn is used, less quantity will be required per yard, but more strands will be needed to fill out our ⅝" width. Test your cord requirements with the one you will use for the tapestry, so that twine can be cut in convenient lengths.

This braid can be made with any odd number of strands in the same manner as for five. There will always be one strand more in one hand than in the other. Regardless of the number, the process is the same.

Keep pull on braid front and center to avoid distortion. Easy tension will result in a fatter braid; hold strands even and only taut enough to control them.

As braid lengthens, move backward to maintain tension; or tie a string and loop about 1" or so above the last few twine passes, and rehang.

For long strips of braid, wrap individual strands around the palm of your hand, slip off the loops so formed, then hold them together with a rubberband around their middle; from the center of the bundle, lengths of twine can be pulled out as needed.

As braiding progresses, the ball ends of the strands will twist in reverse direction; unless they are "cleared" every few inches of braid, a messy tangle can result.

Both faces of the braid are usable when finished. But during the course of its making, use smallish safety pins to mark the top of the braid; should work on a strip be interrupted, it will be easier to pick up again. The bottom of the strip is reversed in twist and direction of passing.

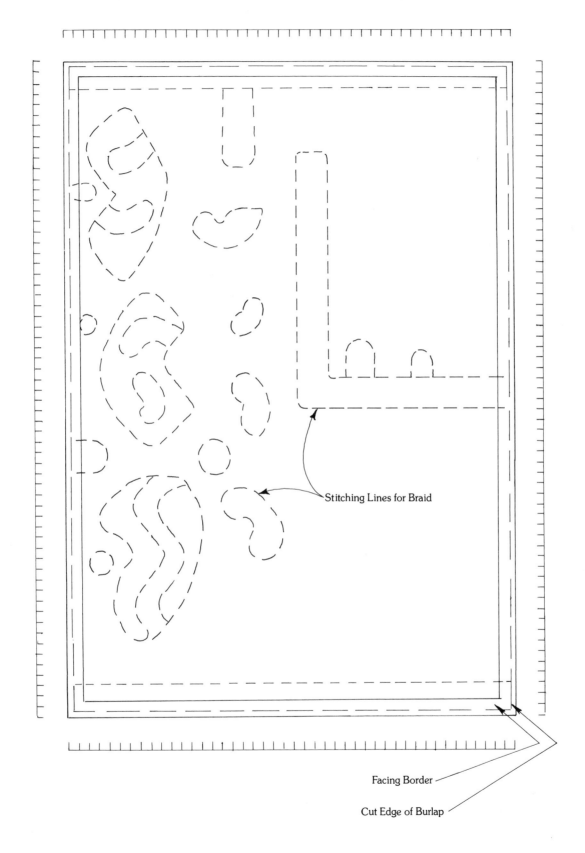

Stitching Lines for Braid

Facing Border

Cut Edge of Burlap

ASSEMBLY

After the design has been enlarged and transferred to the burlap base, measure the perimeters of design motifs and their internal detail. To repeat, work more braid for each unit than seems to be needed. Pin strips to motifs' stitching lines on the burlap, centering them. With carpet thread, neatly back-stitch (top stitching) the braid in place along its center "line."

Where possible, run braid ends out to the burlap edges where they will be covered with the facing; trim them flush. Securely tack loose strands to the burlap margin. In circular or pretzel shapes, one end of braid in effect butts against the other in joining. In this case, before stitching down a strip, with a rug needle run strands of the starting end through to the wrong side. Keep them close together. Stitch through the strand ends to fasten. Pin and stitch braid in place up to the point of joining, overlapping starting end by about ½''; trim. Stitching from side to side through the middle of strands, holding them flat and together, fasten down the end. Then dab the braid ends with glue to further hold them in shape.

In some motifs, one strip of braid will cover the ends of others. In this case, run each strand of each end to the wrong side as for butt joinings, then simply sew covering strip in place. In any case, glueing loose ends of braid will be helpful as long as it dries to a colorless finish.

If the burlap base has not yet been cut to size, do so now. Again secure cut edges with glue about ¼'' in. Cut the lining to 48'' by 66''. Center the burlap face up on the wrong side of the lining and baste in place. Start from the very center of the burlap and stitch diagonally out to each corner. Then baste from top to bottom through the center and from side to side through the center. Be sure the burlap and lining are smooth. Next, baste several horizontal and vertical lines on each side of the center. Last, baste around the four edges of the burlap.

Around the lining, turn ½'' to the wrong side. Fold the lining onto the burlap to form the facing border, which should be about 1½'' wide when finished. Note that there will be about ½'' between the cut edge of burlap and the outside fold of the facing (see diagram) and about 1'' of overlap. Trim the corners to within about 1'' of the fold line. Fold this allowance up, then miter the lining corner onto the burlap. Blind-stitch the miter edges together, then baste the facings onto the burlap all around. With a large-eyed needle and Perle Cotton, Herringbone-stitch the facing to the burlap, going through it to catch the lining with each stitch.

To hang the tapestry, sew rings to the back of the piece along the top stitching line. They should be evenly spaced at about 6'' apart, but there must be one ring about ½'' in from either side edge. For strength, catch up as much fabric in the sewing as possible, without going through to the right side.

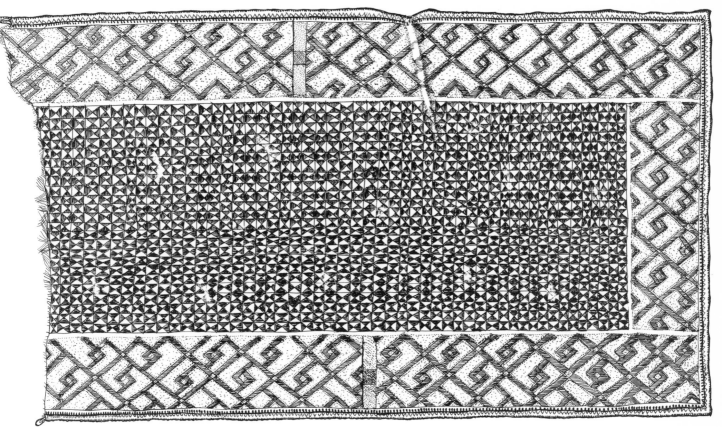

Sketch of typical beaten bark fabric from Zaire,
sewn patchwork probably from a skirt

ZAIRE BARK FABRIC (RUNNER)

This typical beaten bark fabric from Zaire, sewn in patchwork, is probably from a man's sarong, judging by the creases along only one edge of the cloth.

Size: About 57″ in width by 15″ high

Materials: Mono, No. 10 mesh canvas; Persian wool, using full three-thread strand.

This runner is 622 canvas threads across by 158 high. First count out the width and length on the canvas, then mark with a hard pencil or basting thread; then mark the center spaces of the canvas in both length and height the same way. The embroidery is worked across the shorter dimension.

Start at the center to work half of the body panel at a time. Following the diagram, with blue work fifty zigzag stitches from the center toward the left. Turn canvas center line to the bottom to complete the starting row with forty-nine blue stitches, reversing the diagram. Turn canvas center line up again. Now, following the zigzag pattern as established, work across the panel with oatmeal, and continue with alternate rows of blue and oatmeal until there are forty-six rows of each color—thirty canvas threads will remain at the end of the panel. Next, with oatmeal even up the zigzag with fill-in stitches—see diagram.

Across the center of the panel, even up the zigzag in the same way with oatmeal up to the center line. Then, starting with the fill-in's on the other side of the center line, work the second half of the body panel to correspond to the first half, or so that it is a mirror image of the first half.

Surround the completed panel with a band of apricot Flat stitches; as shown in the diagram, it is worked at an angle of 45°, three canvas threads high by three threads wide. Now work the three-square-wide border around the panel, always alternating the color sections as shown. Finish the runner with another apricot band all around.

Did you want another size? For each dimension you will need an odd multiple of eight canvas threads, so that the square pattern will be the same on each of the corresponding sides. Add to those figures six threads more, in all, for the band around the border. Count out the canvas as described above, marking centers. Then, in working the zigzag, stitch to within three threads of the border threads to allow for the inside band of apricot.

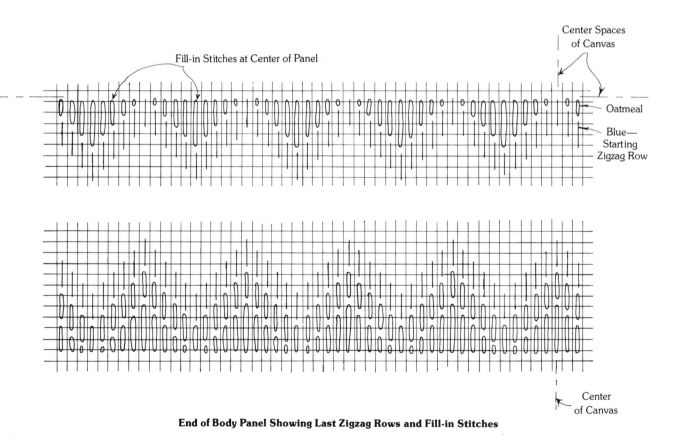

End of Body Panel Showing Last Zigzag Rows and Fill-in Stitches

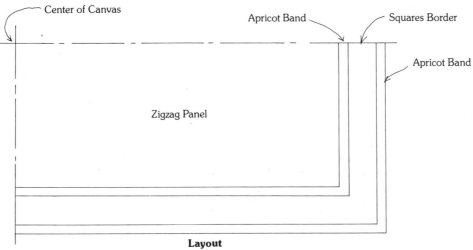

Center of Canvas

Apricot Band

Squares Border

Apricot Band

Zigzag Panel

Layout
Lower-Right-Hand Quarter

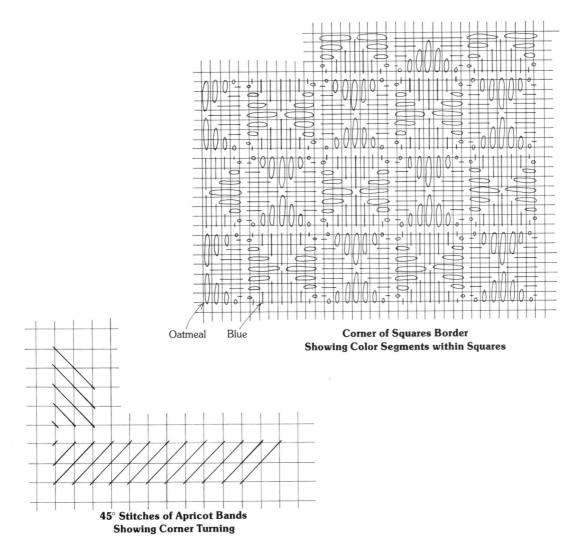

Oatmeal   Blue

Corner of Squares Border
Showing Color Segments within Squares

45° Stitches of Apricot Bands
Showing Corner Turning

Sketch of an Yoruba Adire cloth in the Olokun style.
Cassava paste resist under indigo dye. Author's collection

OLOKUN ADIRE

Originally this Yoruba Adire cloth in the Olokun style was produced by a cassava paste—resist technique under the indigo dye, or painted on and other patterns created from oil-can stencils; either way the artist cannot support himself so we gave him a silkscreen to use. Author's collection

Size: Embroidery is about 15½'' square

Materials: Unfaded blue denim; Persian wool, using two of its three threads at a time, except for French Knots. These are done with only one of the three threads.

The body of the design is divided into 7'' squares, surrounded by a ¾'' border.

Upper-Left-Hand Square: The flower is entirely worked in Chain stitch first. Petal centers are solidly filled with white (A), following the contours from the inner dotted lines toward their centers. Each petal is then outlined with pale blue (B) along the outer dotted lines. Azure blue (C) French Knots fill the flower center. On top of the A Chain stitch, work scattered irregular Straight stitches with C, as shown in the diagram. And, as background for the flower, continue with Straight stitches so that they radiate from the center out to the sides of its square.

Stem Stitch

Satin Stitch

Diagonal Darning—B

All French Knots (o) are in C.

X

Diagonal
Laid Filling
Over Square
Laid Filling

Stem Stitch

Straight Stitches

Chain Stitch

Fly Stitch

Satin Stitch

Satin Stitch

Colors

A—White   B—Pale Blue   C—Azure

Upper-Right-Hand Square: This square is horizontally divided into 7'' by 3½'' rectangles. The upper oblong is further divided into eight squares, alternately filled with B Diagonal Darning and stylized sea horses. Their bodies are worked in Satin stitch—the fine lines in the diagram show the direction of the stitches only. Heads are outlined with Stem stitch, tails are simply Straight stitches. The two left-hand sea horses are stitched in B, the others are C.

In the lower rectangle, C Chain stitch is used for the geometric figure, the rings are B Chain stitch.

Lower-Left-Hand Square: Here the large square is vertically divided into 3½'' by 7'' rectangles. The outer oblong is first filled with Square Laid stitch with A, the tie-down cross bars are done with C. For laid work the cloth should be stretched taut and square on a frame. Starting ⅝'' in from the lower inside corner of the border (X on the diagram), lay on five vertical strands, each ⅝'' apart; as shown in the diagram, the last of these lines will be ⅝'' in from the right-hand edge of this rectangle. Be sure to work with ample ease, so that the fabric will not be puckered when removed from the frame.

Next, starting ⅝'' up from the same corner (Y on the diagram), lay on ten horizontal A strands ⅝'' apart, between the inside border line and the vertical edge of this oblong. The last of these strands will be slightly more than ⅝'' below the rectangle's top edge. A grid of ⅝'' squares has thus been formed. With C, work small slanted tie-down stitches at the crossings of A strands. Since these will be largely covered by next lay-ons, they do not appear on the diagram.

Starting again at X, with A lay on a diagonal strand to Y; continue with lay-ons at this angle (lower-right-hand to upper-left-hand), crossing the corners of the small squares—there will be sixteen strands in all. Then, in the same manner, work sixteen opposite diagonal lay-ons as shown in the diagram. With C and small horizontal stitches, tie down the crossings of the diagonal strands that fall at the center of each ⅝'' square.

To finish the laid work, do C French Knots in each sector of each square. With B Stem-stitch along the right-hand and top edges of the laid rectangle.

The inner oblong of this square is filled with aquatic creatures. Each is first done in Satin stitch, following fine lines for direction of stitches only. Stem-stitch the outline of head and legs of the center turtle. With C overstitch the Satin with Straight stitches, and continue with irregular C Straight stitches to fill in the "sea" background from the laid block to the dash-dot-dot outline of the rectangle.

Lower-Right-Hand Square: Chain stitch is used for all of the spirals—the large pair at upper left and lower right are done with B, the other large pair with C. Smaller spirals are stitched with A.

Around the design squares, there is first a B Stem-stitch line. Between lines of the border, work large Fly stitches—C for side borders, B for top and bottom. Finish the square with C Stem stitch.

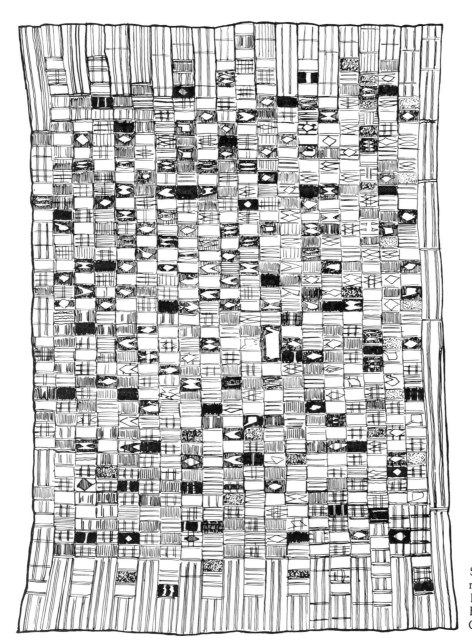

Sketch of a
men's-weave
Kente cloth.
Ewe,
Gold Coast

GOLD COAST KENTE

In this men's weave Kente cloth from Ewe, the ribbons are finger-woven on the most fragile of looms, then overlapped in a Basketweave and sewn along the edges.
Size: About 22″ by 21″
Materials: Mono, No. 10 mesh canvas; Persian wool, using full three-thread strand at a time.

Most of the design is worked in a diagonal Flat Filling stitch; though the length and the width of these stitches vary, they are always at a 45° angle (that is, over the same number of horizontal and vertical threads). Sixteen of the blocks are embellished with Upright Gobelin stitch, some vaguely in the form of fish and animals.

The layout for the upper-left-hand quarter and enlarged detail of the structure of different blocks are shown. Where there is only a color difference between blocks, they are listed below the diagram for the basic block, which shows the different widths, lengths, and numbers of stitches within them.

The lower-left-hand quarter is a mirror image of the upper; the right-hand half "mirrors" the left, except that the colors of A1 and A2, and the E blocks, remain in the same order.

The entire design can be most easily stitched from the upper left downward and toward the right; each color unit within a block can be worked in the same manner.

Upper-Left Quarter

Center

A1	E	A2	E	A1	H	A1
B1		B6		B5		B5
A1	B4	A2	B1	G →	J1	G ←
B1	A1	B6	A1	B8	K	B8
A1	B2	A2	B1	A1	J2	A1
C1	D2	B7	A1	C2	K	C2
D1	B2	A2	B2	A1	J3	A1
B2	A1	B3	F	B5	K	B5
A1	B3	A2	B2	A1	J4	A1
B3	A1	B3	A1	B2	K	B2
A1	B5	A2	B5	A1	J3	A1
B3	A1	B3	A1	B2	K	B2

Center

Center

Center

Basic Block A

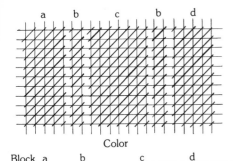

Block	a	b	c	d
			Color	
A1	Gray	Pale Rust	Rose-Beige	Light Brown
A2	Gray	Dark Brown	Rose-Beige	Light Brown

Basic Block B

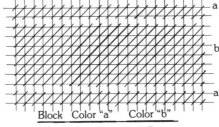

Block	Color "a"	Color "b"
B1	Yellow	Dark Beige
B2	Dark Brown	Light Green
B3	Dark Brown	Yellow
B4	Dark Brown	Red
B5	Yellow	Red
B6	Dark Brown	Medium Green
B7	Yellow	Dark Brown
B8	Yellow	Dark Green

Basic Block C

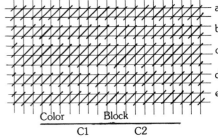

Color	Block	
	C1	C2
a	Rose-Beige	Dark Green
b	Light Brown	Dark Brown
c	Yellow	Yellow
d	Dark Brown	Dark Brown
e	Dark Beige	Dark Green

Block D1

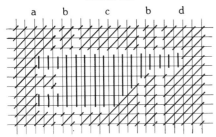

Block D2

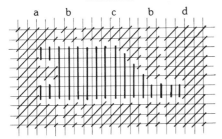

Colors "a" through "d" are the same as for A1. Animals are stitched in eggshell. Reverse facing directions of animals on lower-left-hand quarter; reverse head direction on right-hand side.

Block E

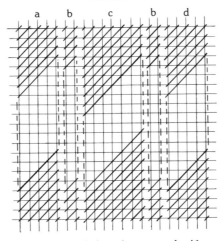

Colors a, b, c & d are the same as for A1.

Block F

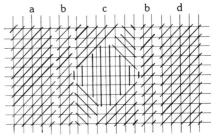

Block G

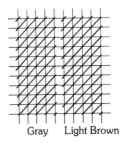

Diamond and fish are eggshell. Colors a, b, c, & d are the same as for A1. Reverse direction of fish on right-hand side.

Block H

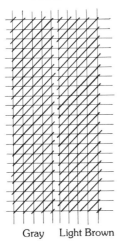

Gray   Light Brown

Basic Block J

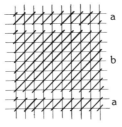

Block	Color "a"	Color "b"
J1	Dark Brown	Medium Green
J2	Dark Brown	Yellow
J3	Yellow	Dark Beige
J4	Yellow	Light Green

Block K

Gray   Light Brown

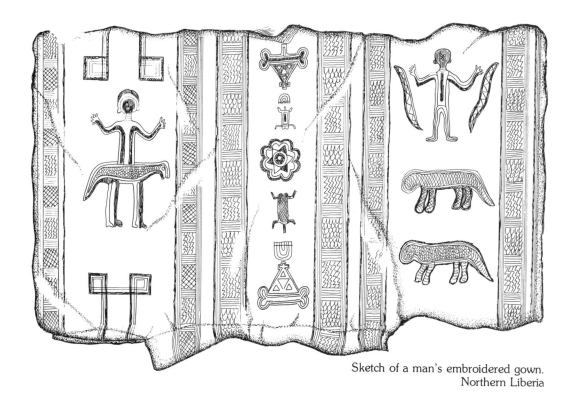

Sketch of a man's embroidered gown.
Northern Liberia

LIBERIAN HUNTER

The embroidery for this man's gown is actually a section of a three-part embroi-
dered panel in thick wool. Liberia (northern)
Size: Embroidery is about 15½'' by 24''
Materials: Unbleached, medium-weight cotton fabric; Persian wool, using one
of its three threads at a time.

Unless otherwise specified, *all* solid lines of the diagram represent slate gray (E)
Split-stitch outlines, and fillings are also done with Split stitch, following the contours
of the various motifs.

The first exception is the top-center figure's head, which is rust (D) Satin stitch
worked in its length. Eyes and nose are eggshell (A) Satin stitch done to cross the D
stitches. Outline them as shown, and the head. Fill in ears with pale rust (B), outline,
and the neck band with A. As shown, each of the B, light rust (C), and D sections of
the body is outlined, and of course the entire figure.

In the serpentine curves on either side of the little "man" comes another exception. Use D and E Satin stitch to fill in the zigzag's triangles, worked perpendicularly
to each outer edge; E Split-stitch the zigzag itself, and around the filled-in triangles.
After bordering them with A on one side, B on the other, outline the entire motif.

Start the topmost beast in its middle, which is Laid Filling. Be especially careful

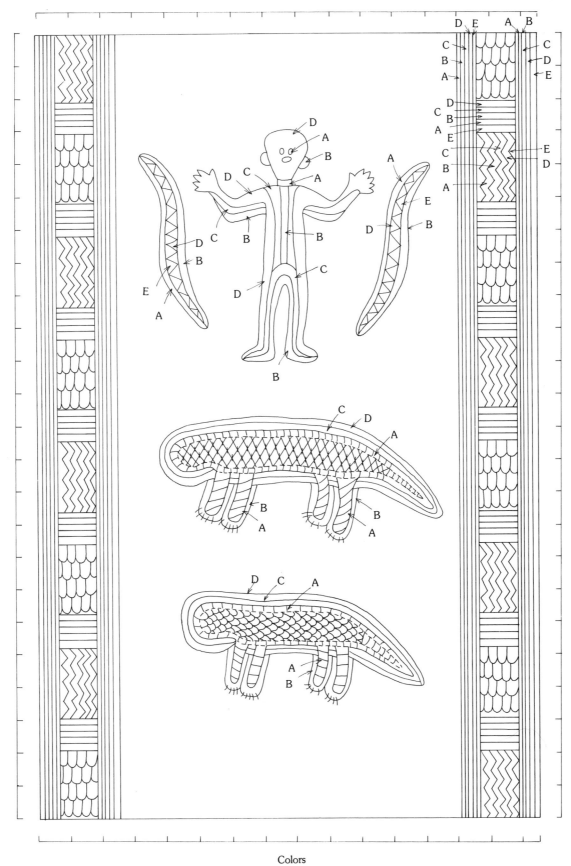

Colors
A—Eggshell B—Pale Rust C—Light Rust D—Rust E—Slate Gray
All solid lines in the diagram are slate gray (E).

about tension here. First lay on the diagonal E lines in each direction, then tie them down at their crossings with short vertical stitches. Starting at the dotted line, there is a narrow A band around the laid work, which is overstitched with E Straight stitches, then outlined. C and D each encircle A, except where legs protrude. Legs are first A filled in with A at their centers (lengthwise). Diagonal lines are E Stem stitch. B borders the legs. Claws are E Straight stitches.

The lower creature is done in the same manner, except for his mid-section. The scale pattern within it is Stem-stitched with E.

Vertical borders on either side of the panel are identical. The wider band at their right-hand edge is E; then come stripes of D, C, B, and A, outlined as shown. In the oblongs, the scale pattern is E Stem stitch. The zigzag is filled in with angled Satin stitch in the same color order as for the stripes. Horizontal bands always start with D at the top, then are C, B, A, and E. Left-hand stripes of the border are done in the same color sequence as for the right-hand series.

The panel can be finished with E outlines at top and bottom edges.

LIBERIAN HORSEMAN

Size: Embroidery about 16½'' by 25''
Materials: Unbleached, medium-weight cotton fabric; Persian wool, using one of its three threads at a time.

Unless otherwise specified, *all* diagram lines are embroidered in slate gray (E) Stem stitch, and fillings are Split stitch, which follow, for the most part, the contours of the design motifs. Embroider the center detail first, then the identical vertical borders on either side.

Center squares of the top pair of frets are E, horizontally stitched; color stripes encircle the square, beginning with eggshell (A), and followed by mauve (B), mulberry (C), and burgundy (D); each stripe and the entire fret are outlined with E as shown.

The center "man-i-mal" is shaded in the same way. His face is vertically stitched E; features are A Satin stitch, on top of and crossing the E. Complete the B, C, and D bands around his head, and B, C, D, and A bands around his neck. Remember, everything is outlined with E. In the same way, stripe the manlike part of the body down to his animal nature.

There, first fill in the entire body center with A, then Stem-stitch the E scale pattern and head detail on top of the A; outline the section. Work the color bands around the body, complete the D legs.

Frets at the bottom of the panel are reversed to correspond to the upper pair.

Working from right to left, the color sequence of each series of vertical stripes is E, D, C, B, and A.

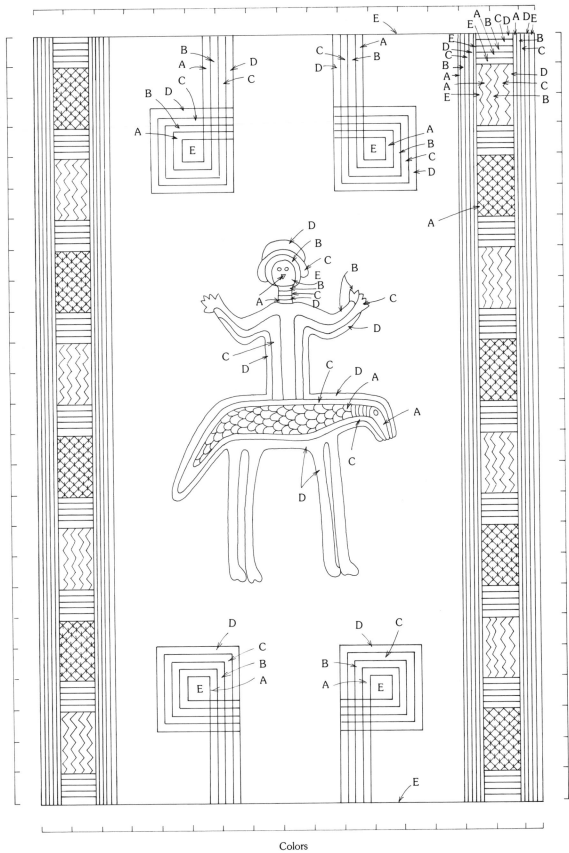

Colors

A—Eggshell   B—Mauve   C—Mulberry   D—Burgundy   E—Slate Gray

All lines of the diagram are stitched in slate gray (E).

Horizontal stripes between the vertical sets are done in Satin stitch, starting with D at the top, then C, B, A, and E, with E outline for each of them as for the verticals.

Zigzag rectangles within the borders are also done in Satin Stitch—this time horizontal—and from right to left are also D, C, B, A, and E. Cross-hatched blocks are first filled in with A (vertically). E diagonal threads are then laid on from upper right to lower left first and are crossed from upper left to lower right. At the crossings of these threads, tie them down with small vertical E stitches.

Top and bottom edges of the panel can be outlined with E to finish the work.

LIBERIAN MASK PANEL

Size: About 13″ from border to border, by 25″
Materials: Unbleached, medium-weight cotton fabric; Persian wool, using one of its three threads at a time.

Unless otherwise specified, *all* diagram lines are slate gray (E) Split-stitch outlines, and fillings are also done in Split stitch, following the contours of the various motifs. Embroider the center motifs first (see enlarged detail for colors), then stitch the identical vertical borders on each side.

Only the features of the conventionalized heads at top and bottom of the panel are filled in with vertical eggshell (A) Satin stitch, and outlined, before covering the center triangle of the face with light gold (B). Continue the heads with dark gold (D) and A bands around the face, then do the "core" of the ears and crown with medium gold (C); encircle that with first D, then A. Remember everything is outlined. In the same way, fill in A at center, D and A again to the topknot of the head. The center of the round-topped "beard" only is vertical A Satin stitch. Partly band it with C and D, then all around with A.

The "flattened" animal forms have diagonal blobs of A Satin stitch at their centers, separated by and outlined with E. Circle the centers with B and C. Next, do the D section of the front-legs unit, and around it a band of A. The heads are vertical A Satin stitch, outlined and "notched" with E. Hind quarters are also D at their center, banded with A. On either side of the bodies between the pairs of legs there are stripes of D on the inside, then A.

At the very center of the panel is a star-centered rosette motif. The center of the motif only is A horizontal Satin stitch, followed by rings of C and D—again, everything is E outlined—and the A star. The scalloped background for the star is B, followed by rings of scallops in A, C, D, and again A.

Work the right-hand series of vertical border stripes next. Start with E—the wider stripe on the outside—then D, C, B, and A, all of equal width. Starting from the top, cross stripes are D, C, B, A, and E, throughout the border. Zigzag oblongs of the border are Satin stitch at an angle. From the right-hand side, begin with B, then

Colors

A—Eggshell   B—Light Gold   C—Medium Gold   D—Dark Gold   E—Slate Gray

See enlarged detail of central motifs for color allocation.

do C, two stripes of D, and E. The alternate oblong's scales are first filled with vertical A Satin stitch; each one is then outlined with E. The left-hand series of stripes follows the color sequence of the first set.

The panel can be finished at top and bottom edges with E outlining.

Sketch of Kwame Nkruma wearing his Kente cloth robe against a background
of men's weave Akan, Ghana. Collection of Jack Lenor Larson, N.Y.

KENTE CLOTH

This is a sketch of Kwame Nkruma wearing his Kente cloth robe against a background of men's weave. Akan, Ghana Collection of Jack Lenor, Larson N.Y.

Size: About 20½'' by 20''

Materials: Mono, No. 10 mesh canvas; Persian wool, using full three-thread strand.

Five broad vertical stripes are crossed at irregular intervals with narrow bands of contrasting stitch and color, for this woven effect. Done mostly in Horizontal and Upright Gobelin stitch, the entire design covers 218 canvas threads across and fills 211 spaces high.

The work can be started at either upper corner, completing each stripe section and crossband in turn, without rotating the canvas for the different directions of the stitches (unless so desired); the Continental stitch stripes are worked vertically from top to bottom, too.

Lower-case letters denote the colors used within a particular space; numbers that follow upper-case letters indicate the height of a stripe section; the numbers of stitches are listed in the chart that accompanies the diagram for that section.

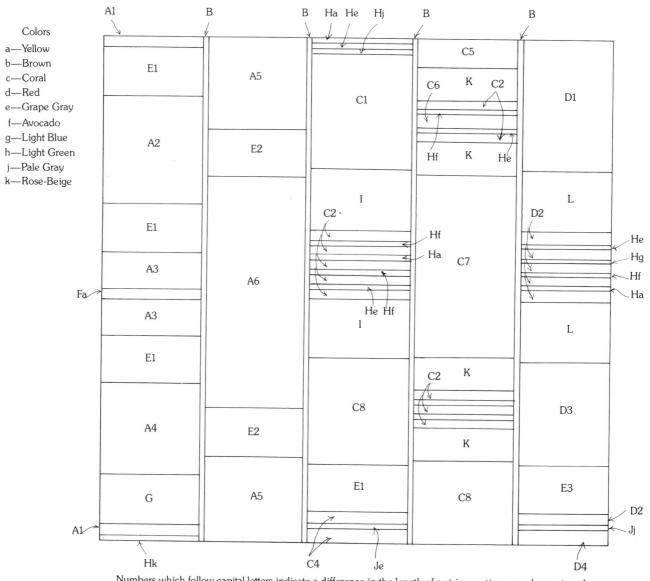

Colors
a—Yellow
b—Brown
c—Coral
d—Red
e—Grape Gray
f—Avocado
g—Light Blue
h—Light Green
j—Pale Gray
k—Rose-Beige

Numbers which follow capital letters indicate a difference in the length of a stripe section or a change in color. See detail diagrams. Lower-case letters indicate a particular color.

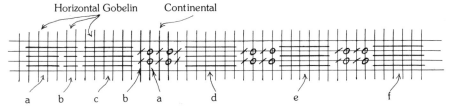

Horizontal Gobelin   Continental

a   b   c   b   a   d   e   f

Vertical Stripe A

A-1	5 Stitches High	A-4 40 Stitches High
A-2	46 Stitches High	A-5 37 Stitches High
A-3	16 Stitches High	A-6 96 Stitches High

Horizontal Gobelin

Vertical Stripe B

211 Stitches High

b

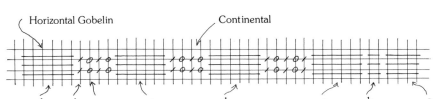

Horizontal Gobelin   Continental

f   b   a   e   d   c   b   a

Vertical Stripe C

C-1	49 Stitches High	C-5 13 Stitches High
C-2	5 Stitches High	C-6 7 Stitches High
C-3	45 Stitches High	C-7 18 Stitches High
C-4	4 Stitches High	C-8 32 Stitches High

Cross Stripe E

Upright Gobelin
g (j-g)

c (c-d)

Byzantine
h (k-c)

c (c-d)

g (j-g)

Lower-case letters are colors for E-1;
Letters enclosed () are for E-2 and E-3.
E stripe is the same width across
as A and B.

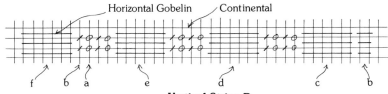

Horizontal Gobelin   Continental

f   b   a   e   d   c   b

Vertical Stripe D

D-1	56 Stitches High	D-3 46 Stitches High
D-2	5 Stitches High	D-4 6 Stitches High

Cross Stripe H

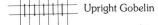 Upright Gobelin

Cross stripe F is the same as H but
is stitched over four horizontal threads.

All Upright Gobelin

g
c
h
d
c
g

Cross Stripe G

All Upright Gobelin

j
f
b
a

All Upright
Gobelin

e

a
b
f
j

Cross Stripe I

Upright Gobelin

a
f

Scotch
Stitch

f
a
f
a

Cross Stripe K

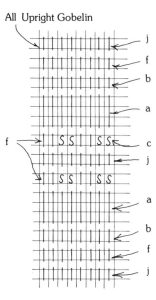

All Upright Gobelin

j
f
b
a
c
j
a
b
f
j

Cross Stripe L

Sketch of Royal Fon costume, appliqué and embroidery. Dahomey

FON APPLIQUÉ

This design is from a Royal Fon costume from Dahomey, appliquéd with embroidery that holds down the clover designs in a very ingenious way.

Size: About 15″ square

Materials: Mono, No. 10 mesh canvas; Persian wool, using full three-thread strands.

This design is worked in horizontal and vertical Straight stitches of varying widths. Though not shown in the diagram for clarity, the red and oatmeal borders encircle the work. A one-way stripe pattern (dotted lines on the diagram) forms the entire background for the red and oatmeal motifs.

Except for the background, the lower-right-hand quarter of the design is the reverse of the upper; the entire left-hand side is the reverse of the right.

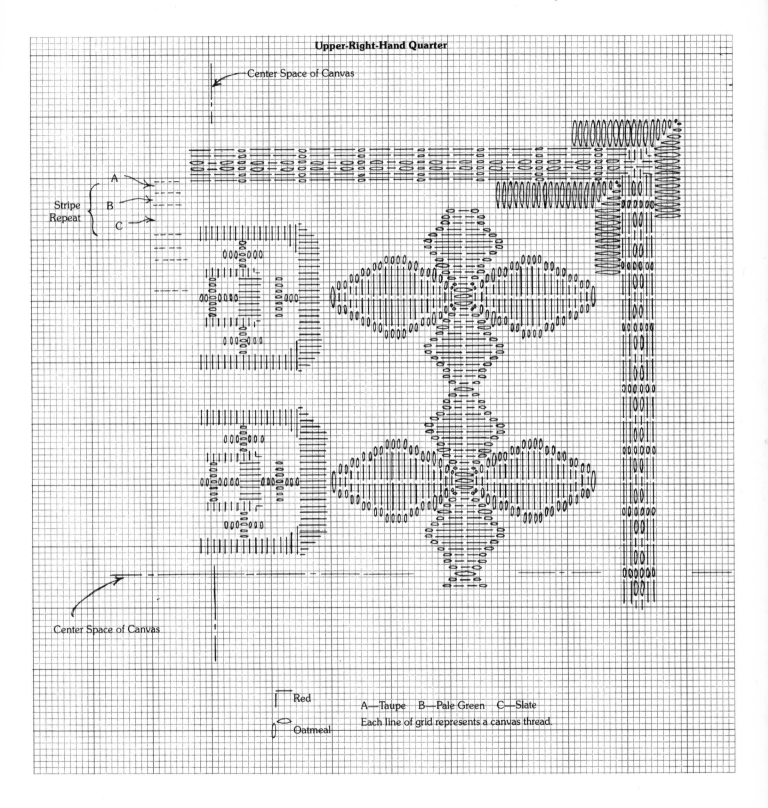

Upper-Right-Hand Quarter

Center Space of Canvas

Stripe
Repeat

A
B
C

Center Space of Canvas

Red

Oatmeal

A—Taupe   B—Pale Green   C—Slate

Each line of grid represents a canvas thread.

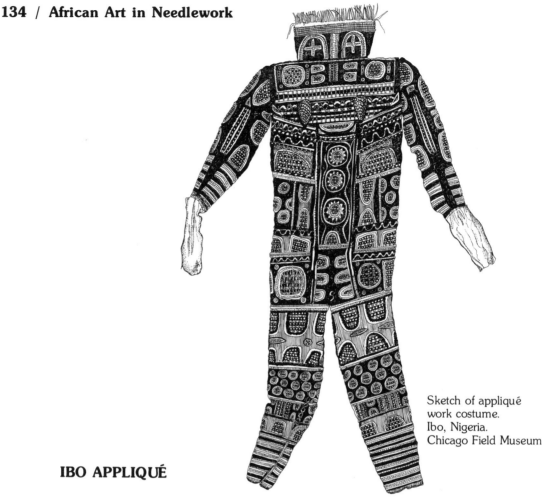

Sketch of appliqué
work costume.
Ibo, Nigeria.
Chicago Field Museum

IBO APPLIQUÉ

This design is typical of many I saw appliquéd on garments throughout Nigeria.
Field Museum, Chicago
Size: About 15″ by 16″
Materials: Mono, No. 10 mesh canvas; Persian wool, using full three-thread
strands.

Straight stitches, both horizontal and vertical, make up this design. The check
patterns are similar to Interwoven stitch in their formation. The larger blocks are four
stitches worked over five canvas threads, each horizontal row in alternating colors.
The small checks, which form the centers of the mid-section motifs, are stitched in
the same manner but are three sets wide and worked over four canvas threads. The
horizontal-stitch blocks can be worked in vertical rows, the vertical-stitch blocks in
horizontal rows, skipping the necessary number of canvas threads and spaces. Thus
one color is filled in at a time. Though not completely shown for clarity, the red and
pale green borders surround the work.

The diagram shows the upper-right-hand quarter. The design reverses for the
lower quarter; the left-hand side is the reverse of the right, except that the checks are
always in the same color order.

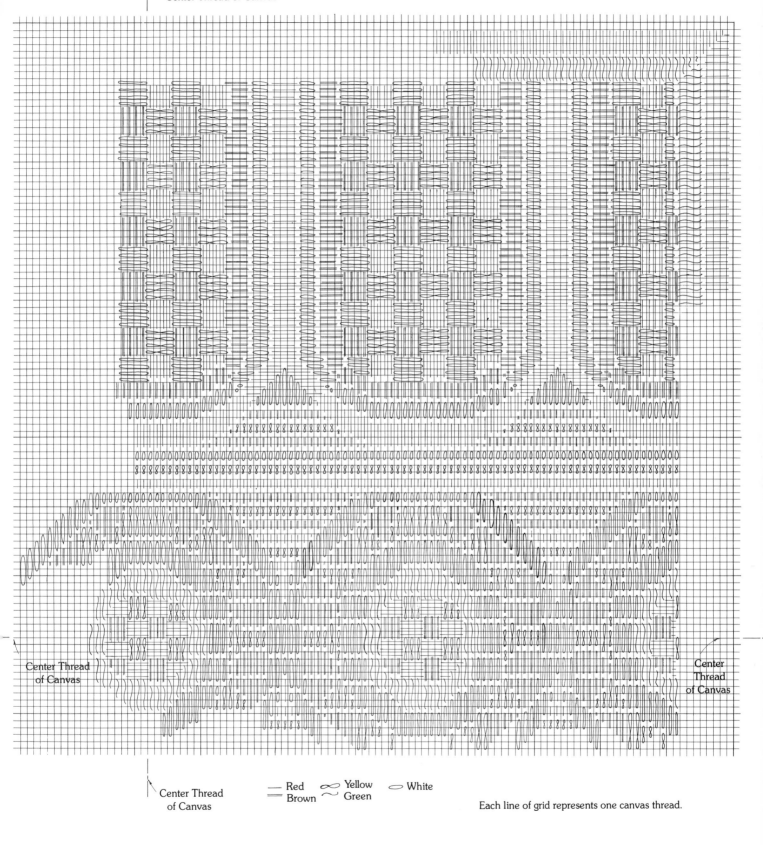

Center Thread of Canvas

Center Thread
of Canvas

Center
Thread
of Canvas

Center Thread
of Canvas

— Red   ∞ Yellow   ◡ White
= Brown   ∿ Green

Each line of grid represents one canvas thread.

Index

Africa, map of, to embroider, 43–45
African art, xiii–xiv
Akan designs, 98–107
  elephant, 107
  fish, 104
  hand, 102–103
  heart, 103
  lizard, 106
  for quilt, 98–102
  wheel, 105
Alternating Mosaic stitch, 16
  used in leopard spot pattern, 68
American Museum of Natural History,
    xiii, 46
Appliqué, 99–100
  uses of:
    Ibo costume, design from,
      134–135
    Royal Fon costume, design from,
      132–133
Arm band, ivory, 70

Background fabric, to cover, 54
Bag, beaded, design from, 76–77
Bargello, 10, 14
  used in leopard spot pattern, 68

Bark fabric, 113
  pattern from, 113–115
Basketweave stitch, 17
  ending of threads in, 9
  uses of:
    Akan designs, 104–107
    beaded bag, design from, 76
    beaded cuirass, design from, 78
    Benin head design, 46
    bronze plaques, designs from,
      48–58
    Congo dance mask design, 82
    double purse, 73
    elephant pillow, 107
    fish designs, 56, 58, 104
    flower design from bronze plaque,
      52
    fringe design from bronze plaque,
      50
    Lagos rug, 80
    leopard design, 66
    leopard spot pattern, 68
    lizard pillow, 106
    Nigerian puff, 70
    sarong pattern from bronze plaque,
      48
    wheel pillow, 105

Basketweave stitch: uses of (cont'd)
    white slaver design from bronze
      plaque, 54
Beaded bag, design from, 76–77
Beaded cuirass, design from, 78–79
Benin bronze plaques, 48, 50, 52, 54, 56
  designs from, 48–59
Benin head, bronze, 46
  design from, 46–47
Benin leopard, ivory, 66
  designs from, 66–69
Bias-cut fabric, to embroider, 4
Blanket stitch, 22
Blixen, Karen, Baroness Blixen-Finecke,
    Out of Africa, xiv
Blocking of embroidery, 7–8
Braid for Kuba wall hanging, 109–110
Brass polish, to clean needles, 6
Brick stitch, 28–29
  uses of:
    fish design from bronze plaque, 56
    cheetah skin pattern, 96
Bronze plaques, Benin, 48, 50, 52, 54,
    56
  fish designs from, 56–59
  flower design from, 52–53
  fringe design from, 50–51
  sarong pattern from, 48–49
  white slaver design from, 54–55
Bronze portrait head, 46
Bronze rooster, 64
  designs from, 60–65
Burlap fish wall hanging, 58–59
Burlap fishscales, 59
Bushman cave murals, xiv, 84
Bushman hunt design, 84–86
Butterfly designs:
  giraffe patterned, 92–93
  leopard patterned, 94–95
  zebra patterned, 90–91
Buttonhole stitch, 22
  uses of:
    African map, 43
    Akan quilt, 99
Byzantine stitch, 30–31

Canvas, 4
  counting of threads of, 4, 9
  stretching of, 5
Carbon for transfers, 7
Carved temple door, rubbing from, 80
Cassava paste–resist technique, 116
Cave murals, Bushman, xiv, 84
Center of work, to locate, 9
Chain stitch, 20
  uses of:
    burlap fish wall haning, 58
    giraffe patterned butterfly, 92
    Olokun Adire, 116, 118
    as padding, 33
Cheetah in Kenya, 94
Cheetah skin pattern, 96–97
chief's fan, 88
  design from, 88–89
Circles, to draw, 6
Cleaning of embroidery, 8
Colorfastness of materials, 4, 8
Colors of thread, sequence of use, 10
Congo dance mask, 82
  design from, 82–83
Continental stitch, 10, 17, 18
  ending of thread in, 9
  uses of:
    Akan designs, 104, 105
    beaded bag, design from, 76
    beaded cuirass, design from, 78
    Benin head design, 46
    bronze plaques, designs from,
      48–55, 58
    Congo dance mask design, 82
    double purse, 73
    fish designs, 58, 104
    flower design from bronze plaque,
      52
    fringe design from bronze plaque,
      50
    Kente cloth pattern, 130
    Lagos rug, 80
    leopard design, 66
    Lesotho leaf pattern, 86
    Nigerian puff, 70

Continental stitch: uses of (*cont'd*)
  sarong pattern from Bronze plaque, 48
  wheel pillow, 105
  white slaver design from bronze plaque, 54
Cotton thread, 4
Couched filling stitches, 37—38
Couching stitch, 35
  used in African map, 43, 44
Counted thread embroidery, 5, 25
Counting of canvas threads, 4, 9
Crewel work, cleaning of, 8
Crib quilt, 98—102
Cross stitch, 25—27
  used in fish design from bronze plaque, 56, 58
Cuirass, beaded, design from, 78—79

DMC Perle Cotton, 4
DMC Six Strand Embroidery Cotton, 4
Dahomey, Royal Fon costume from, 132
Daisy stitch, 29
Dance mask from Congo, 82
Darned filling stitches, 36
Designs:
  enlarging of, 6
  sources of, xiii
  transferring of, 7
Detached chain stitch, 29
Diagonal darning, in rooster design, 64
Direction of stitch, 9
Direction of work, marking for, 9
Double purse, Nigerian, 72—75

Edges of fabric, 8, 9
Elephant pillow, 107
Embroidery, 3
Encroaching stitches, 33
  uses of:
    giraffe patterned butterfly, 92
    zebra patterned butterfly, 90
Ends of threads, 9

Enlarging of designs, 6
Ewe, Kente cloth from, 119
Eye of needle, 4

Fabrics for embroidery, 4
  amount needed, 9
Feather patterns, 60—61, 64
  frame, 62—63, 64
Field Museum, Benin, Nigeria, exhibits:
  bronze plaques, 48, 50, 52, 54, 56
  bronze rooster, 64
  chief's fan, 88
  Ibo garment, 134
  ivory leopard, 66
Field Museum, Chicago, Ill., xiii
Field stone decorated hut, Lesotho, 86
Filling stitches, 36—38, 118
  darned, 36
  flat, 15
  laid, couched, 37—38
Fish:
  Akan pillow design, 104
  Benin bronze plaque, 56
    designs from, 56—59
  burlap wall hanging, 58—59
Fishscales, burlap, 59
Flame stitch, 14
Flannel, red, 88
Flat filling stitch, 15
Floating of threads, 9
Florentine stitch, 14
Flower design from bronze plaque, 52—53
Fly stitch, 32
  used in Olokun Adire, 118
Fon appliqué design, 132—133
Frames, 5
  feather design for, 62—63, 64
French knots, 39
  uses of:
    African map, 44
    burlap fish wall hanging, 58
    chief's fan design, 88
    Olokun Adire, 116, 118

Gauges:
   of canvas, 4
   of needles, 4
Giraffes in Kenya, 92
Giraffe patterned butterfly design,
      92–93
Glue, for edges of fabric, 7, 8, 9
Gobelin stitch, 13–15
   uses of:
      Gold Coast Kente, 120
      Kente cloth design, 130
Gold Coast Kente, 119–121

Hand panel design, 102–103
Hassock, 70–71
Heart pillow design, 103
Herringbone stitch, 23
Hoops for embroidery, 5
Horizontal Gobelin stitch, 14
   used in Kente cloth design, 130
Horseman, Liberian, 124–126
Hunter, Liberian, 122–124
Hut in Lesotho, 86

Ibo appliqué design, 134–135
Interfacing, 4
Interwoven stitches, 19
   uses of:
      Lesotho leaf pattern, 87
      white slaver design, 54
Ironing of embroidery, 8
Ivory arm band, 70
Ivory leopard carving, 66

Joan Moshimer pattern pencil, 5

Kente cloth, 119, 129–131
Kenya:
   cheetah in, 94
   giraffes in, 92
   zebra in, 90
King's sarong, from bronze plaque, 48
Knitted fabric, to embroider, 4
Knots, 9
   See also French knots
Kuba raffia panel, 108–112

Lagos rug design, 80–81
Laid filling, couched, 37–38
   uses of:
      Liberian hunter design, 122–124
      Olokun Adire, 118
Laundering of embroidery materials, 4,
      8
Lazy Daisy stitch, 29
   used in African map, 43
Leaf pattern, 86–87
Length of stitches, 33
Lenor, Jack, 129
Leopard design, 66–67
Leopard patterned butterfly design,
      94–95
Leopard spot pattern, 68–69
Lesotho:
   cave murals in, xiv, 84
   Rondavel hut in, 86
Lesotho leaf pattern, 86–87
Liberian embroidered panel, 122
   horseman design from, 124–126
   hunter design from, 122–124
   mask designs from, 126–128
Lizard pillow, 106

Map of Africa, to embroider, 43–45
Markers, 8
Mask designs:
   Congo, 82–83
   Liberian, 126–128
Masking tape, 6, 9
Mosaic stitch, 15–16
   uses of:
      fish design from bronze plaque, 58
      leopard spot pattern, 68
Moshimer, Joan, pattern pencil, 5
Museum of Modern Art, xiii
Museum of Natural History, xiii, 46

Napkins, paper, 6
Neck strap for double purse, 73–74
Needles, 4–5
   brass polish to clean, 6
Nigerian beaded bag, design from,
      76–77

Nigerian beaded cuirass, design from, 78–79
Nigerian double purse, 72–75
Nigerian puff, 70–71
Nkruma, Kwame, 129

Oblique Gobelin stitch, 15
Olokun Adire, 116–118
Organdie, 4
  for transfers, 7
Ornithoptera giraffícus, 92–93
Out of Africa, Blixen, xiv
Outline stitch, 21
  used in Bushman hunt design, 84, 86

Paper towels, 6
Papilio zebrancus, 90
Paternayan Persian wool thread, 4
Pattern pencils, 5
Pens, 8
Perle Cotton embroidery thread, 4
Photostat, enlarging of design by, 6
Pillows, Akan designs for:
  elephant, 107
  fish, 104
  heart, 103
  lizard, 106
  wheel, 105
Pins, 8
Polygonia leopardus, 94–95
Portuguese slaver, 54
Pressing of embroidery, 8
Purse, double, 72–75

Quilt, Akan designs for, 98–102

Raffia panel, design from, 108–112
Red flannel, 88
Rippers, 5
Rock face, Bushman painting on, 84
Rondavel hut, 86
Rooster, bronze, 60, 64–65
  feather patterns, 60–64
Royal Fon costume, 132
Rubbing from carved temple door, 80
Rug pattern, 80–81

Running stitch, 3
  used as padding, 33

Sarong pattern, from bronze plaque, 48
  fringe pattern from, 50
Satin stitch, 33
  uses of:
    African map, 43, 44
    Akan quilt, 99–100
    Bushman hunt design, 84, 86
    giraffe patterned butterfly, 92
    leopard patterned butterfly, 94
    Liberian horseman design, 124, 126
    Liberian hunter design, 122, 124
    Liberian mask panel, 126, 128
    Olokun Adire, 118
    rooster feather pattern, 64
    zebra patterned butterfly, 90
Scissors, 5
Scotch stitch, 23–24
Seam rippers, 5
Sethslabatebe, Lesotho, xiv, 84
Shadow work on sheer fabrics, 23
Sheer fabrics, 4
  shadow work on, 23
  for transfer of design, 7
Single-journey method of Cross stitch, 26
Slanted satin stitch, 33
Sources of designs, xiii
Split stitch, 34
  uses of:
    African map, 43
    Akan heart pillow design, 103
    Bushman hunt design, 84
    chief's fan design, 88
    giraffe patterned butterfly, 92
    Liberian horseman design, 124
    Liberian hunter design, 122
    Liberian mask panel, 126
    as padding, 33
    zebra patterned butterfly, 90
Square Laid stitch, used in Olokun Adire, 118

Stem stitch, 21
uses of:
African map, 43, 44
Akan heart pillow design, 103
burlap fish wall hanging, 58
burlap fishscales, 59
Bushman hunt design, 84, 86
chief's fan design, 88
giraffe patterned butterfly, 92
leopard patterned butterfly, 94
Liberian horseman design, 124
Liberian hunter design, 122
Olokun Adire, 118
rooster feather pattern, 64
zebra patterned butterfly, 90
Stitches, 11–39
Alternating Mosaic, 16, 68
Bargello, 14, 68
Basketweave, 9, 17, 46, 48, 50, 52,
54, 56, 58, 66, 68, 70, 73, 76,
78, 80, 82, 104, 105, 106, 107
Blanket stitch, 22
Brick stitch, 28, 56, 96
Buttonhole stitch, 22, 43, 99
Byzantine stitch, 30–31
Chain stitch, 20, 58, 92, 116, 118
Continental stitch, 9, 10, 17, 18, 46,
48, 50, 52, 54, 58, 66, 70, 73,
76, 78, 80, 82, 86, 104, 105, 130
Couching stitch, 35, 43, 44
Cross stitch, 25–27, 56–58
Darned filling, diagonal, 36
Encroaching Satin stitch, 33, 90, 92
Filling stitches:
Darned, 36
Flat, 15, 118
Laid, 37
Flame stitch, 14
Flat filling stitch, 15, 118
Florentine stitch, 14
Fly stitch, 32, 118
French knots, 39, 44, 58, 88, 116,
118
Gobelin stitch, 13–15, 120, 130
Herringbone stitch, 23

Stitches (*cont'd*)
Horizontal Gobelin stitch, 14
Interwoven stitch, 19
Laid filling, Couched, 37–38, 122
Lazy Daisy stitch, 29, 43
length of, 33
Mosaic stitch, 15–16, 58, 68
Oblique Gobelin stitch, 15
Outline stitch, 21, 84, 86
Satin stitch, 33, 43, 44, 64, 84, 86, 90,
92, 94, 99–100, 118, 122, 124,
126, 128
Scotch stitch, 23–24
Split stitch, 33, 34, 43, 84, 88, 90, 92,
103, 122, 124, 126
Stem stitch, 21, 43, 44, 58, 59, 64, 84,
88, 90, 94, 103, 118, 124
Straight stitches, 10, 16, 30, 43, 44,
56, 58, 94, 116, 118, 124, 132
Tent stitch, 17
Tie-down stitches, 37, 38
Upright Cross stitch, 26–27
Upright Gobelin stitch, 13, 120, 130
Wide Gobelin stitch, 15
Straight stitches, 10, 16, 30
uses of:
African map, 43, 44
fish design from bronze plaque, 56,
58
Fon appliqué design, 132
Ibo appliqué design, 134
leopard patterned butterfly, 94
Liberian hunter design, 124
Olokun Adire, 116, 118
Strands of thread, use of four, 54
Strap slides for double purse, 73
Stretchers for embroidery fabric, 5

Tacks, 8
Tapestry needles, 5
Tassel design from bronze plaque, 50
Temple door, rubbing from, 80
Tension, 3, 5
Tent stitch, 17
Textured fabric, to embroider, 4

Thimbles, 5
Threads:
   counting of, 9
   for embroidery, 4
   ending off of, 9
   floating of, 9
   number required to cover back-
      ground, 54
Tie-down stitches, 37, 38
Transferring of designs, 7
   for hassock, 70
Tufting of Akan quilt, 100
Twist of thread, 3

Upright Cross stitch, 26–27
Upright Gobelin stitch, 13–14
   uses of:
      Gold Coast Kente, 120
      Kente cloth, 130

Wall hangings:
   burlap fish, 58–59
   Kuba raffia panel design, 108–112
Wheel pillow, 105
White Slaver design, 54–55
Wide Gobelin stitch, 15
Wide Stem stitch, 21
Wool thread, 4

Yoruba Adire cloth, 116

Zaire:
   bark fabric from, 113
   raffia panel from, 108
Zebra in Kenya, 90
Zebra patterned butterfly, 90–91